Grasp the Situation

Grasp the Situation

Lessons Learned in Change Leadership

Glenn H. Varney, PhD
Scott Janoch, BSC
James M. McFillen, DBA

GRASP THE SITUATION

iUniverse books may be ordered through booksellers or by contacting:

iUniverse
1663 Liberty Drive
Bloomington, IN 47403
www.iuniverse.com
1-800-Authors (1-800-288-4677)

Because of the dynamic nature of the Internet, any web addresses or links contained in this book may have changed since publication and may no longer be valid. The views expressed in this work are solely those of the author and do not necessarily reflect the views of the publisher, and the publisher hereby disclaims any responsibility for them.

Any people depicted in stock imagery provided by Thinkstock are models, and such images are being used for illustrative purposes only. Certain stock imagery © Thinkstock.

ISBN: 978-1-4917-6721-4 (sc)
ISBN: 978-1-4917-6720-7 (hc)
ISBN: 978-1-4917-6722-1 (e)

Library of Congress Control Number: 2015911009

Print information available on the last page.

iUniverse rev. date: 07/20/2015

Dedicated to all
those who have
learned the lesson
of how to
grasp the situation
before they make change

Contents

Preface

The inspiration for this book occurred during a recent housecleaning when I came across some old consulting project files. Perhaps you can understand how hard it was to put them down. I just couldn't resist the temptation to look through them and reminisce about the good old days. As I scanned through the files, I noted that a number of the projects had been less than successful.

Like a lightning bolt, I was struck by a common characteristic among the projects: there were always one or two leaders who championed their approaches to change by pushing their solutions to the problems. They would say, "We just don't have time to stand around and contemplate. We need to fix it now." They looked at the situation, quickly came to a conclusion about what action needed to be taken, and fired their cannons at what they perceived to be the problem.

When I studied and reflected upon each case, the evidence pointed squarely at the failure of the people involved (both leaders and consultants) to understand the circumstances surrounding the problems. No one took the time to diagnose the situation in order to fully identify what was going on and what needed to be changed. They simply started throwing out solutions, hoping they would somehow hit the target. As a result, such actions often caused damage to careers, to departments, and, in some cases, to entire organizations.

As I read through my files, I began to see where the ship had been steered in the wrong direction, where my clients' leaders created mistakes. My pride and self-confidence took a hit from this humbling review of my so-called expert advice, but I licked my wounds and decided that it might be helpful to share these mistakes to offer lessons to leaders, consultants, teachers, students of change, and others who might find themselves in positions of leadership. Thus the idea for this book was born.

I use a storytelling technique to communicate with you. The use of stories to convey ideas and lessons predates recorded knowledge. Lessons about life were passed on by word of mouth in the form of stories. Today, information and much of our learning come to us via computers, smartphones, social media, and so forth. We believe that great speakers are great teachers because they know how to tell true stories that highlight the learning they wish their audiences to take home and use.

This book, with its true stories of organizational change efforts, recounts my career over a span of about forty-five years, from working for a large chemical company, through going back to school, teaching at a university, and then owning a consulting firm for thirty years before retiring.

During this period, the other coauthors, Scott and Jim, had a major impact on my way of approaching organizational change. Scott entered the picture when I took on a major change project with an Italian-owned company. Scott was corporate director of labor relations and compliance and was primarily involved in the company's union relations.

Jim was a professor of management and consultant in the same university where I served as a professor. He influenced my view of how to effectively change organizations when we worked together teaching an organization development course using the Leading Organizational Change story presented later in this book. In all but two stories, I am the storyteller, with Scott and Jim helping to put the stories into useable form.

Finally, you might be interested in how I came up with the book title, *Grasp the Situation*. A good friend of mine, Dave LaHote, told me that if I used the phrase "organization diagnosis" in the title, it would turn off readers. He suggested using "grasp the situation" instead, which is a term used by advocates of lean manufacturing for organizational diagnosis.

We hope you will grasp the situation behind the writing of this book and benefit from our lessons learned. Perhaps you can steer your own ship into smoother waters.

Glenn H. Varney
Scott Janoch
James M. McFillen

Introduction

Understanding what needs to be changed in any organization before you design and install an intervention to correct a problem sounds logical. The reality is that a large number of changes are implemented with little to no evidence or facts that define what needs to be changed. Result: failure and/or redesign that is costly and wasteful.

This book is designed to share with you how grasping the situation (what needs to be changed) can save you time and money.

If you follow a five-step change process for making large and small changes in organizations, your change success rate will be high, and you will actually make money because your intervention will work instead of failing or only bumping along with a change that causes more problems than it solves. Here are the five steps, briefly:

1	2	3	4	5
Recognizing the Problem →	Collecting and Synthesizing Relevant Symptoms →	Formulating a Preliminary Diagnosis →	Testing the Preliminary Diagnosis →	Intervention Design

Throughout this book, we will help you learn how to follow these steps by explaining the concepts and providing real-life stories that show where the steps weren't followed and then describing the resulting consequences.

As you read each story and transition through the five steps, the stories might not seem to progress in a straightforward, linear manner. This is because some mistakes made in previous projects were repeated in subsequent projects. Learning is not always smooth; sometimes it takes more than one try to get it right.

This book is chronological, beginning with my experience with the chemical company, progressing through my work with Scott on a major change project, and concluding with teaching how to lead organizational change with Jim.

As you read this book, you'll learn four lessons about change in organizations that will benefit you in your own change efforts:

1. Successful change is in the eye of the beholder. Rarely can you claim complete success. Most of the time you will have some parts of the change process that work and others that do not. Some success is better than none at all.
2. Beneficial change (i.e., improving something and making it work better) requires a clear and complete analysis of what is not working in the manner that you want it to work.
3. All change interventions must be tested before implementation to assure their validity (i.e., that they actually do what they are supposed to do and they do it reliably, working properly time after time).
4. Change leaders—an organization's CEO, president, and executives—are capable of

championing change, but they rarely apply their scientific process skills in making change.

You might be asking yourself, "Why should I read any further, and just exactly what will I get out of this book?" Well, there are several benefits for you if you keep going.

First, for business students, teachers, managers, and all types of leaders, this book will help you make changes and implement changes that work.

Second, we hope you find the stories informative and helpful in making change.

Third, we hope this book will arouse your hidden scientific talents and you'll learn how to use these talents to make changes, at work and in your personal life, that work.

Read on and enjoy!

If you are interested in a more technical description of the five-step diagnostic approach to change, you can also read the article we published in the *Journal of Change Management*, "Organizational Diagnosis: An Evidence Based Approach."

Awareness
Phase I

Glenn H. Varney, PhD

How I Learned to
Grasp the Situation

Early in my career, following receipt of my MBA from The Ohio State University, I went to work for a large paint manufacturer. I had worked at this job for about a year and a half when I was called into my supervisor's office and told that my services were no longer needed. When I asked why, I was told that my job was being eliminated. I later found out that my boss didn't think I had the smarts to solve the problems facing the company. I had no idea what I lacked in "smarts," and I thought it was the company's loss, not mine.

I found a good job in human resources with a small company where I believed that my efforts were paying off because I had introduced several new programs and systems that people liked, and they told me that I had helped solve some of the problems the company was facing.

After two and a half years (by then I was four years out of school and twenty-eight years old), I took a new position working for a large chemical company. My duties were to record and track the company's organization and staffing charts. The company president at the time was a former army general, and he was big on "tables of organization." I have to tell you it was one boring job. For the life of me, I could not see how what I was doing had any impact on the performance of the organization. In fact, I thought it caused a drag on the company. Within about a year, the president retired, and a member of the principle owner's family took on the top position of CEO/president.

At this point, things really started to change; he wanted

a new HR function for the company that showed interest in the development of human resources. This brought a new opportunity for me. I was offered the position of college recruiting and management development. I took on this job and expanded the company's college-recruiting program to a point where we were getting an acceptance rate of one out of every three offers. This meant we were bringing in a steady stream of talented engineers and chemists, thus providing a large pool of talented potential leaders. We matched these young graduates with the best-of-the-best senior leaders in the company to develop leaders for the top positions in the organization.

I kept working with the company, and ten to twelve years later, we found a large number of these people in key management positions. In the meantime, we had been busy conducting management development training programs designed to improve the performance of the present management, to prepare them for promotion to more senior positions. All of our management development activities and programs were based on the following guides for effective management:

- Build a strong organization by selecting and developing outstanding people.
- Follow sound organizational practices.
- Communicate to all levels within the company.
- Develop an atmosphere for creativity.
- Instill the importance of profits in the minds of all employees.
- Develop short- and long-range plans and strategies.
- Measure results against predetermined standards of performance.
- Keep the overall company point of view clearly in mind.
- Present a good image of the company to all employees and the public.
- Conduct business with integrity.

About eight years into my employment, my boss, the vice president of human resources, assigned me the task of assessing the retirement situation for the top leadership staff in the company. What we found in our study shocked the president. We were going to lose sixteen members of our twenty-five-member Management Advisory Council (MAC) within ten years! The following caricature drawing was used to awaken the sleeping giant:

The drawing was designed based on actual retirement data and actuarial death/illness rates. The remaining members of the MAC were all within five years of their normal retirement dates.

The drawing worked, and the organization and its leaders began to prepare Individual Development Plans (IDPs) for high-potential midlevel managers. During the next five years, most of those for whom we developed IDPs moved upward in the organization. However, much to our dismay, the older, talented managers, in whom the organization had heavily invested, were not moved upward to higher-level positions. Instead they were being passed over for the new, young college recruits. What a blow; we had poured millions of dollars into management development with little to no return on the investment. This failure led to the following conclusion:

> Management development in a large number of organizations tends to be relatively ineffective—and in some cases a counter-productive process that, in fact, might be doing an immeasurable amount of damage to the organization. Oftentimes management development (MD) tends to be based on the notion that "if it's education, it has to be good." Usually in such cases the investment in MD produces results which

are not measured and often turn out to be the opposite of those intended.

—An Organization Development Approach
to Management Development, 1976,
Addison-Wesley

What I learned from this experience was to get people to grasp the situation by whatever means necessary.

After twelve years with the chemical company, I accepted a new job with a small chemical compounding company as the senior HR officer. I was probing around for a graduate program when I was introduced to the PhD program in organization development at Case Western Reserve University. Faculty and students told me that the field of organization development (OD) had the answers to organizational improvement because it used a systematic approach to change. I was convinced that this was for me, so I quit my well-paying job and entered the PhD program at the ripe old age of forty.

The lesson learned from my work experience in industry is quite simple; I realized that good ideas are easy to sell, but implementing them in real-life organizations requires scientific skills. After returning to school, I learned how to make successful changes at work and in my personal life.

Back to School
Phase II

Back to School:
Learning How to Learn

After fifteen years away from the books, I jumped in with both feet and started back to school. What a shock! I had given up a high-paying job, with two kids and a wife to support, and in addition, I had to pay my own tuition. Many of my friends told me that I was crazy and that I would never make it, either financially or in successfully completing my degree. Thankfully, my wife went back to work part time, and I had a friend who helped me get onto the lecture circuit so that I could make ends meet.

Being back in the classroom was a trial, but once I got into the swing of things, it became an uplifting experience. I was opening up my mind to new ideas, thought processes, and knowledge about how to change myself and how to help others change. A couple of things lodged squarely in my stubborn brain:

First I realized that real, sustainable change depends on whether or not the people required to make the change buy into the change. *People make change work because they see how it will benefit them and their fellow employees.*

Second, I learned that making change that sticks and works to improve organizations must be skillfully understood and designed based on the nature and character of the change. *You had better have a clear picture of what and why you want to change before you design an intervention.*

Being back in school offered me the opportunity to develop relationships with many thought leaders in organization development, including the likes of George Odiorne, Chris Argyris, Frank Friedlander, and many others. What an enlightening experience it was to design change processes with people like Bob Golembiewski, Craig Lundberg, and others, all founding experts in change management. In addition, I got acquainted with many practitioners who claimed to be on the cutting edge of change. In one case, I was invited to participate as an instructor in a large change project working with a well-known change expert.

I learned an interesting lesson from a so-called change expert who, for the purposes of this writing, I have named Brock Fielding.

Story 1—The Legend of Brock Fielding

Brock Fielding was a consultant who became enamored with a problem-solving program he had designed, and he sold this same prepackaged program to each of his clients regardless of its impact on the client's organization. Brock believed that his ideas would work for everyone. He never tried to find out what the client's real needs were, and he gave no thought to testing the viability of his program. He was the embodiment of the old saying: "When the only tool you have is a hammer, you tend to treat every problem like a nail."

In the not too distant past, Brock Fielding had an enlightening experience. Brock, like many change practitioners, had entered the field of organizational development (OD) with an educational background that wasn't related to organizational change. He graduated from a large Midwestern university with a bachelor of arts degree, followed by an MBA, and finally by a PhD in recreational management.

His first job out of school was as a city park recreation

specialist with the Parks Department of a small Ohio city, but he soon became disenchanted with the lack of advancement opportunities. A college buddy of his, Porter Black, had become a recognized change agent, and he encouraged Brock to look into the field of organization development. Porter told Brock that if he was interested in OD, he needed to attend a national conference where he could "meet the folks" already in the field. Porter also recommended that Brock attend one or two seminars so that he could learn the basics needed to help organizations improve their human relations. These actions, according to Porter, would enable Brock to help clients enhance the work experience for the people in their organizations. Brock was assured that improving employees' work lives always leads to better, more productive organizations.

Brock attended a national conference where he met many change practitioners who gave him advice on how to get started. In addition, he completed two one-week-long workshops and was presented with a Certificate of Satisfactory Completion, which authorized him to practice change management in all types of organizations.

Soon thereafter, Brock quit his job with the Parks Department, printed new business cards identifying himself as *Dr. Brock Fielding, Consultant in Organizational Change Management*, and hung out his shingle. The first few years, he struggled to make ends meet. Then one day, after completing an outdoor event with a small client, he had an awakening. It dawned on him that one of his programs, a one-day training session he called Engaging in Change (EIC), really excited people. He decided to focus his practice on this program because people seemed to love it.

Now, Brock was no dummy. He had done his homework and based his program on a viable hypothesis:

> *If you engage people and seek and use their ideas to build commitment, it leads to their support of change, which in turn results in the organization becoming more productive.*

Brock was encouraged to continue selling his Engaging in Change program because he got rave reviews following each event. He concluded that since people liked it, they would use it.

Before too long, Brock began to make a name for himself. His practice had really taken off, and he was attracting a growing client base. Then one day he received the following letter:

Dear Dr. Fielding:

My name is Charles Clausen. I am the Plant Manager of Render Parts Company—a supplier to major automotive manufacturers. My plant is located in Finley, Ohio. I just returned from a conference where I heard about your work and would like to talk to you regarding running your one-day EIC session in my organization. Please call or email me if you are interested.

Sincerely,
Charles Clausen

Brock wasted no time in calling and arranging a visit to the plant. Clausen told him he had discovered, while attending an automotive conference, that American workers in Japanese-owned facilities were highly productive and happy because they worked in teams and small groups. He asked Brock if training his 120 supervisors in the Engaging in Change program would be a way to develop teamwork in the workplace. Brock assured him that the EIC program would result in happier employees and increased plant performance. Clausen was sold, and he encouraged Brock to submit a proposal.

Brock was delighted; he was doing quite well financially, but he could smell the big contract. *My goodness*, he thought, *120 supervisors x $250 for the one-day session = $30,000. In addition, Render Parts Company has ten other plants to which I can expand my program, provided I do well in Clausen's plant.*

With no hesitation, Brock agreed to write a proposal with a deadline for completing six one-day sessions. With twenty supervisors in each session, he could train all 120 supervisors during the plant's two-week annual changeover shutdown period. True to his roots in the recreation industry, he scheduled the training offsite in the local city park. The training was completed on time, and a high percentage of the 120 supervisors expressed satisfaction with program. A large number said they would apply the team concept with their employees. The word spread throughout Render Parts Company, and five of the company's other ten plants expressed interest in having him conduct his EIC program at their locations.

The supervisors in Clausen's plant returned to work

energized and began to apply the simple formula that Brock had taught them:

Engaging Employees + Seeking Ideas
= Building Commitment =
Productive Organizations

The plant supervisors, as they had been taught by Brock, frequently pulled small groups of workers off the production line to talk to them about working smarter and increasing production, and they required all workers to come in to work twenty minutes early twice each week for EIC sessions. After three months, they calculated that they had about 50 percent employee involvement. Then one day a brusque announcement was issued by the company's management (not Clausen): "All EIC activities are to cease immediately!"

The announced reason for this abrupt cancellation of EIC activities was the identification of some interesting metrics in Charles Clausen's plant:

- The plant's efficiency rate had dropped 15 percent.
- Union grievances had increased 40 percent.
- Employee tardiness was up 30 percent.
- An attitude survey reported a sharp decline in worker confidence in management/supervision.

Overall, the company estimated that Clausen's plant had sustained a $1 million loss during the previous quarter, and top management blamed the Engaging in Change program. There was no attempt to look for other causes that might have affected these numbers.

The word soon spread to the company's other locations,

and Brock's involvement with Render Parts Company was abruptly terminated. *Oh well*, he thought, *I made a good buck, and there are plenty more organizations out there that I can tap.*

The Rest of the Story

Brock's program was cancelled in all of Render Parts Company's plants. Some were abruptly discontinued just days before training was scheduled.

In one plant, they had expanded the program to a two-day session, which was cancelled at the end of the first day with no explanation. The information about the performance results in Clausen's plant sent a chill down the spines of all of the plant managers.

Brock managed to keep his practice alive, but word of his experience at Render Parts Company started to get around. New contracts dropped sharply, to a point where he had only two or three programs scheduled during a three-month period compared to as many as four per week in good times. Brock began looking for a permanent job in some organization.

An Early Lesson in Grasping the Situation

This Clausen project clearly failed, but what made this a good learning experience for me was that, for the first time, I was on the delivery side of training. In my past employment, I had hired trainers to teach people things I thought they ought to know, with little or no regard to whether or not they needed training, and with no thought about whether or not they were receptive to training.

Witnessing Brock in action clearly taught me that just standing in front of managers and supervisors, telling them how to become engaged in change, with not the slightest idea of whether or not they needed or wanted to be engaged in change, was futile. It was like talking to a blank wall. The only time I got the sense that participants were engaged in the process was when they were playing a game, like Desert Survival; then they would perk up and show some interest. The evaluations they completed were always good, probably because participating meant getting away from their daily routines, and critical evaluations tell management that the training isn't working.

So what Brock was doing was entertaining, not teaching. They loved it, but they didn't learn from it. I learned three things from watching Brock in action:

1. Training must be designed to change a behavior or skill, and it should be done in such a way that participants see the value to themselves personally as well as to their organizations.
2. All training and educative processes should be based on a "need for change" study (diagram) that clearly defines what changes are needed.
3. Training should be designed (intervention) based on what needs to be changed.

During this period, I was also going out on the lecture circuit, and most of what I was doing was entertaining managers and supervisors to keep them from getting bored. I entertained in order to get good evaluations and to encourage the organizations to keep sending people to my presentations. However, following my experience with Brock Fielding, I began to pose the following questions

Glenn H. Varney, PhD

to attendees at the beginning of each training session I conducted:

1. Why are you here?
2. What do you want to take home with you today?

Most of the answers were similar to the following:

1. I was told to attend.
2. I don't know why I'm here, so I don't know what I'm supposed to take home with me.

This early lesson taught me *not to expect people to be receptive to learning if they don't feel the need to change something they are comfortable doing.*

Because Brock Fielding did not grasp the situation, he failed. He had no sense of the needs of his students and the impact his training would have on them. He should have engaged them at the start to see how well his training fit their needs.

I hope you'll like the next story, which occurred about a year after my experience with Brock Fielding—it will ring bells and remind you of people you know or have met in the past. As you read this story, ask yourself if you would want to work for a person like Mike, or what you would do if Mike were your boss. I worked for Mike while I was in school. Knowing what I know now, even if I was desperate for money (and I sure was in those days), I would never take on the job of helping him figure out why "my staff isn't able to handle simple problems."

Story 2—Don't Ever Become a Mike "Fix-It"

This is a story about the plant manager of a five-hundred-employee operation in a small town near Detroit, Michigan. The plant manufactures body-trim parts for several of the major automobile companies. Mike, the plant manager, is an engineer who has been with the company for twenty-two years. His management style can best be described as "if it's broken, fix it."

I met with Mike at his request several days after the events outlined in this story. He called me in because, in his words, "I am damned upset; my staff doesn't seem to be able to handle a simple problem. I always have to step in and fix everything. I want to know what is going on and why my staff can't get it done."

Mike didn't understand why his staff couldn't seem to solve problems and why it was always up to him to be the problem solver in his organization. Here, in his own words, is Mike's story:

"I had just approved the lease of a new multifunctional Xerox machine, which allowed all reports to be printed at three stations. This enabled us to reduce the number of individual printers in the plant. This was an increase of one machine over the existing two older multifunctional machines. Justification for the additional machine was that it would enable the plant to meet the increased 'work load' and eliminate 'wasted time.' One machine was located in the plant while another was in the second-floor office area, where my office is also located. The third machine was to be placed in the first-floor production scheduling location, which is an open office area.

"One day, about three weeks after the new machine had

been installed, I jumped out of my chair and announced to my assistant, 'I'm going out in the plant.' It was my custom to make unannounced spot checks on the operations. This time, I was checking on the operation of the new Xerox machine.

"I headed for the production scheduling area to observe (from a distance) the activity around the Xerox machine. What I saw, when I looked toward the plant, was several people lined up to use the old copy machine. I thought to myself, *This looks like it did before we acquired the new machine—the staff is still wasting time and using the machine as a social center.* Then I turned to observe the new Xerox site. There I saw a group of six employees milling around talking to each other with pieces of paper in their hands. With considerable self-restraint, I walked away mumbling to myself, 'I added an extra machine, and the decision was totally wrong. It's costing me thousands of dollars a month, and nothing has gotten any better.'

"I headed back to my office, passing the second-floor Xerox machine (the one near my office) and noted that no one was using that machine. When I got back to my office, I called my assistant in and told her to call Xerox and have the new first-floor machine taken out. The machine was removed, and guess what? Lines began to form again at the second-floor machine. I could only conclude one thing: people are making up items to run off just so they can socialize, gab, and churn the rumor mill.

"I was determined to get this problem solved, so I sent an e-mail to all managers announcing that in the future each department should appoint one representative to run the department's copies during an assigned period. They were also instructed to call ahead to make sure the machine was available, thus avoiding gossip and social gatherings.

"A few days later, I made another trip into the plant, *Wow!* I thought. *It's working—no one is standing around the copy machines anymore.* However, during the next regular weekly staff meeting, I learned that production was still behind schedule. My management team explained that production reports were still not getting out on time and that we were continuing to experience production delays. I told Glenn Varney, 'This is why I called you in. I need to get to the root of this problem.'"

The Rest of the Story

My first reaction was to tell Mike that he was causing his own problems. His impulsive drive to fix whatever he saw not working the way he thought things should work was the core of most of the problems in his organization. He saw something he thought was not working the way it should work (a symptom), he jumped to a conclusion about what the solution should be (install a new copy machine), and he took action.

Because I was pretty sure that Mike wouldn't listen to me, I took a less direct approach. I decided to collect some background information on the following events (symptoms) in hopes that the facts would be more persuasive in helping Mike understand what was actually happening in his organization. So I took a look at

- the justification for a new Xerox machine;
- why this new machine was placed in the first-floor production scheduling area;

- why people were lined up at the new machine (in Mike's opinion, "wasting time and using the new machine as a social center");
- how people felt about the removal of the new machine just a few weeks after its installation and why they returned to lining up at the second-floor copier just like they had done at the new machine; and
- what the impact of Mike's directive to "assign one person to run each department's copies and to schedule the use of the machine" was on the attitudes and work output of his employees.

I received approval from Mike to talk to his staff and to those people he had classified as "wasting time and using the machine as a social center." This is what I learned:

- The justification for the new Xerox machine had been based on a conversation that Mike's administrative manager had with a Xerox salesman. The salesman presented documentation from other companies showing significant savings if individual printers were removed and a central printing station was provided to handle all the printing. The salesman forgot to mention networking in his rush to install a new piece of equipment.
- The new machine was placed in the production scheduling area because this location had available space. In addition, the scheduling manager claimed that "this is where most of the reports are generated."
- People lined up around the machine because fifteen individual printers had been removed from

throughout the plant and the new printer/copier was the only place where reports could be printed. The two other older machines had been designated for local use only.

- The impact on staff was dramatic, and what people were talking about in line was how "stupid" and "wasteful" the whole idea was. Productive time had been turned into delays and complaints. The whole process had created a wave of discontent throughout the plant.

- With Mike's final edict, requiring departments to schedule the use of the Xerox machine on the second floor, staff members became utterly frustrated and unhappy about the situation. They blamed management (Mike) for the entire problem.

In a nutshell, this problem occurred because of a decision based on *no* data justifying the change. Installing a new Xerox machine and eliminating the individual printing stations only compounded the problem.

Because Mike was the person at whom the finger of blame was pointed, I decided to confront him with the facts. I held a meeting with him, reporting the results of the study, exercising care not to use direct quotes about Mike's decision being "stupid" and "wasteful." Mike didn't ask any questions; he simply listened with no expression on his face. When I was finished, Mike said, "I appreciate your advice." (I really hadn't given him any.) "Now I know what to do, and I will take it from here."

I left feeling that I hadn't really connected with Mike and that the problem would not be solved. Several weeks after the reporting meeting with Mike, I called him to see how things were going. He explained that he had taken care of the problem by firing his administrative manager. It is doubtful that Mike changed or that he will change his fix-it method of problem solving.

Grasping the Situation after the Fact

This incident was a huge failure for me, but it also occurred early in my change management career. It was a very valuable learning experience. Looking back, Mike's opening comments blaming his staff should have been a clue that part of the blame was Mike's. So what did I take away from this experience? I learned to *always formulate a hypothesis about the problem based on a preliminary scan performed at the outset. Signals (symptoms) will guide you in your study and help to provide facts/data that will precipitate change in the client.* I also learned that *before agreeing to work for a client, you should conduct a preliminary scan of the problem to incorporate in your contract proposal. This will signal to the client the direction you plan to take and provide an early warning of the possible outcome of the study. Be sure to formulate your hypothesis in everyday words, and look for signs of a problem, like how the employees felt about Mike (recognizing the problem). Then develop an idea of what is going on (what is Mike doing) and check it out to see if that is really what is occurring.*

Story 3—A Clash of Cultures

In the next story, I was working with a good friend who was the vice president of human resources. He had been responsible for building a new plant using all of the latest organizational theories and practices, including self-directed work teams, open-space offices, zero defects, and so forth. His company had hired a young plant manager who was right in step with these organizational concepts. My role was to help this new plant manager fine-tune his operation focusing on high performance, customer satisfaction, and employee engagement. As a beginner in change management, I couldn't have asked for a better opportunity to learn. This is an example of how it was done correctly but almost went off the track anyway.

The business was an aging, family-owned, small auto parts business located in southern Indiana. The owners built a new high-performance plant designed to take advantage of the technology available at the time, and the management vowed to treat employees fairly and to remain nonunion. The new plant was performing very well, and employee attitudes were high because they were all committed to making sure the new design actually worked.

The founder and CEO of the business contracted cancer and suddenly died, leaving the project in disarray and passing the operation of the plant to his son. After struggling unsuccessfully to keep the plant profitable and the workers employed, the company was eventually sold to a large French auto parts conglomerate. This story recounts what actually happened following the takeover by the French.

The French Assume Control

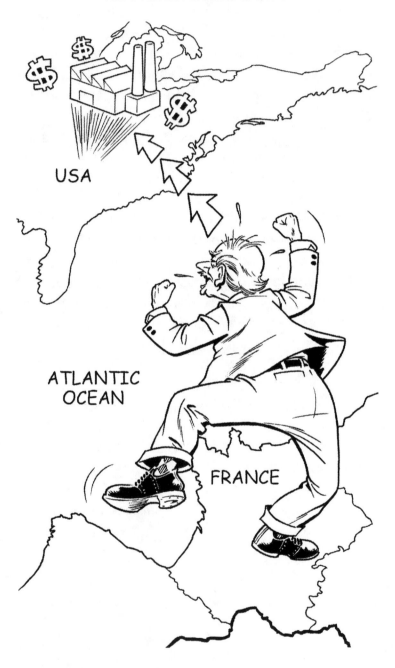

As soon as they assumed control, the first thing the new French owners did was to remove the old leadership team and recruit a new plant manager, William "Bill" Fontly. Bill had gained his experience working for a well-regarded American manufacturer of household appliances. The new owners told him that they expected cost reductions, improved quality and productivity, lower inventories, and so forth, and they gave him six months to deliver. Unfortunately, during that six-month period, the auto industry experienced a major sales slump that also depressed the auto parts business. Two of the companies to which the plant supplied parts cut back on orders and stretched out delivery dates, making it impossible for Bill to meet the demands of the French owners.

When the six months Bill had been given were up, the French company sent a vice president from the corporate office in Paris to give Bill new marching orders. He was instructed to lay off 30 percent of the workforce, eliminate all overtime, and reduce fixed costs by at least 10 percent. They even directed him to cancel the third shift, explaining, "You don't need a night shift; we never force our employees to work at night."

Bill was shocked at this list of demands, and he responded, "How can you, with no understanding of how this operation works, come in here and try to tell us how to run our plant? I'll get you the 10 percent cost reductions, and more, but I'll do it my way. You can either accept that, or you can have my resignation right now."

The vice president was stunned at being spoken to this way by a "brash American." After a few moments of shocked silence, he said, "I will report your comments to my superiors, and you can be sure that you will be hearing from corporate headquarters." The vice president returned to France, leaving Bill expecting to be terminated within a few days. But Bill didn't wait for the ax to fall. Instead, this not-so-ordinary plant manager decided that action was needed.

With my advice and assistance, Bill formed a study group composed of supervisors, hourly workforce members, supply chain staff, an engineer, and a customer service representative to dig into the plant's problems. The stimulus for self-diagnosis was clear to everyone— the life of the plant and all of their jobs were at stake. While Bill waited to hear from the French, the study group spent about two weeks researching the plant's situation.

Their study revealed three critical factors:

- Eighty-five percent of the plant's business came from only two customers.
- Their equipment was modern, but the physical production layout was inefficient.
- The employees were highly motivated and wanted to help save the plant and their jobs.

Although they identified a number of other opportunities for improvement, these three offered the greatest potential for improving the plant performances during the sales slump.

Four weeks after the vice president visited the plant, Bill received a terse e-mail from the corporate office. It read: "You must reduce your costs by at least 10 percent in the next two months. We will review your performance at the beginning of the next fiscal year in January." Bill took this to mean that he had been given the go ahead to do it his way, and, with all lingering doubts removed, his study group went forward with renewed vigor.

Cross-functional teams were formed to study and make recommendations for changes in the supply chain process and for implementing other efficiency improvements. They also tackled the "two customers = 85 percent of the business" problem. In order to reduce the plant's dependence on these two customers, the team members created a customer study team to explore the potential customer base. Hourly employees and other plant personnel contacted various auto-related businesses to demonstrate how they could provide products that would help those organizations reduce their cost and improve quality and delivery requirements. After three weeks of effort, the customer study team was responsible for landing a "trial order" to supply modular radiator units to a European auto manufacturer who was building a new assembly plant in the area. This new business replaced more than half of the production that had been lost when their two major customers cut back on what they had been ordering.

The study teams also recommended changes in plant scheduling and layout, which, after being implemented, resulted in a reduction of 20 percent in the processing time for each unit manufactured. The highly motivated workforce suggested reducing the standard workweek from forty hours to thirty-five hours until the crisis was over. In addition, many workers volunteered to take leaves of absence or use their vacation time to reduce the number of employees on the floor during each of the three shifts.

By the end of the two-month period, the combined effects of all of the changes had produced a cost reduction of 21.8 percent. The plant's business plan for the following year called for an additional 15 percent reduction in cost, with no reduction in customer deliveries. Bill never heard another word from the French corporate office. He and all of the employees understood that they had succeeded in saving the plant and that they were on track for a great future.

The Rest of the Story

Bill can best be described as a strong leader of people who believed that the human resources of an organization are the ones most qualified to diagnose problems and improve performance. The French, on the other hand, displayed an autocratic leadership style that restricted performance improvements by creating resistance to change. Imagine what would have happened if Bill had simply followed orders. If the plant had surrendered to the corporate office dictates, the employees would have been demoralized, and performance would have dropped even further.

Thanks to Bill and the plant's workforce, the plant emerged from the downturn as the second-best performer in all of the French company's organization. It became the primary supplier for two other plants operated by the company, and hopefully the French learned something about managing employees in the American work environment. To this day, the employees have found no reason to seek union representation.

Grasping the Situation after the Fact

When the French acquired the company, my role as advisor to the original plant manager ended, and I thought I was out of work. Not entirely true! The French-hired plant manager began a dialogue with me regarding the way the plant was designed to operate. He liked the plan and intended to keep operating the plant as it was originally set up. Then along came the French, and it looked like all of that good work was going down the tube. But thanks to Bill's resistance and disobedience to his French manager, the plant succeeded. So what did I learn from this experience?

- Most of the new organizational concepts and practices worked in the greenfield operations.
- Strong leadership is required to resist the pull to follow traditional organizational practices.
- Organizations that acquire existing operations need to understand the culture of the new organization to be sure that they do not destroy the greatness of the acquired organization.

What made this a great learning experience for me was the realization that new organizational concepts and practices work when care is used in setting up a new organization. Furthermore, *I realized the importance of diagnosis when acquiring an established operation.*

The next story comes from working with a good friend who was vice president of service operations for a large banking equipment company. I had known Bob before going back to school, and this provided me with work, learning (school), and a practice opportunity that not all students are afforded.

Story 4—Get the Facts before You Act

A business leader had information flying at him from all directions. His problems began when he reacted to the symptoms of a problem before he collected all of the facts in the situation. As a result, he wasted time and ended up with many very unhappy employees. Here is Randy's story, in his own words.

"My name is Randy Daggett. I am the director of customer equipment service for a large US banking equipment manufacturer. Our company manufactures ATM machines, voting machines, and other related equipment. I am responsible for making sure that the customer gets immediate service response to equipment breakdowns anywhere in the United States. I supervise a staff of thirty-two dispatchers working twenty-four hours per day, seven days per week, out of the company headquarters in a small city in Ohio. I am directly responsible for fifteen service call stations that are staffed by twenty female dispatchers on day shift and six more on each of the second and third shifts. My call to service response time is excellent, and my proficiency rating is well above average. Here's my story and what I learned.

"I arrived at work about thirty minutes late on a cold Tuesday morning in January. Normal starting time is 8:00 a.m., but that morning traffic was bad, and I got stuck behind a school bus. As I headed down the hall toward my office, the third-shift lead person, Jane Bruning, breezed by me. She seemed upset. She glanced at me reproachfully and then said in a low voice, 'Damn, I'll be late picking up Johnny to take him to school.'

"As I passed the Customer Equipment Services Department, I noted that Rachel Beam, my first-shift lead person, was there, and everyone was at their work stations. When I reached my office and took off my coat, I noticed a note pinned to the back of the chair that read "Randy, call the boss ASAP, Rita."

I wondered what that was all about, but then I saw a telephone slip on top of my Do Today pile, which read:

> For: Randy
> Date: today
> Time: 8:25 a.m.
> Phone call from Robert Black, HR Director.
> Message: Call me when you get in.

"Now I was getting concerned. Then I noted that I had a large number of e-mails on my computer, and three were work related. Two didn't seem to require immediate action, but one caught my attention. It was from the office union representative, Bob Grieverman. It read:

> To: Randy Daggett
> Subject: A problem in your department
> Date: Tuesday, 8:31 a.m.
> From: Bob Grieverman
> Call me on my cell phone, 891-4328, as soon as you get in.

"I made a quick check of my calendar and saw that I

had an interview scheduled for 10:00 a.m. and a luncheon meeting with my boss at 11:45 a.m. at Rachel's Bistro. Just as I was deciding what to do first, the telephone rang. It was Rose Brushman, one of my first-shift dispatchers.

"She sounded distressed. 'Can I meet with you as soon as possible? I need to explain something to you.'

"I told her that I would have to call her back in a little while and then I hung up. As I took a deep breath, I couldn't help thinking, *What a way to start the morning!*"

The Rest of the Story

"Noting that Jane was very upset when she left work, I figured that something had happened on the third shift. With the other calls from the union representative and the HR director waiting, I decided that I would delay calling my boss because I thought the call probably had something to do with the 11:45 a.m. lunch meeting that I was scheduled to attend. I thought to myself, *I can't contact Jane, but I bet Jane's frustration as she left work is related to the call from Rose Brushman*, so I decided to contact Rose first.

"When I reached her by phone, she sounded very upset, and she said, 'Can I see you right now?'

"I told her, 'Come on over to my office. I will be waiting for you.'

"To my surprise, she showed up with Bob Grieverman, her union representative. Before I could ask what this was all about, Bob said, 'I am here to represent Rose in her unfair treatment by the third-shift lead person, Jane Bruning.'

"After hearing the details of the complaint, I concluded that Rose had been about fifteen minutes late for work.

Jane had had to stay at work to fill in for Rose, which made her late departing work to pick up her son. Rose claimed that Jane had yelled at her and threatened to get her fired. This was the protest the union representative lodged at the meeting. I told them I would look into the matter and get back to them before the end of the shift.

"Then I went directly to the office of Robert Block, HR director. Robert said, 'We have an out-of-control situation with the union. They are accusing management of mistreating Rose. I have already talked to some other employees, including Rachel Beam, Rose's day-shift lead person. They all witnessed the event, and they reported that Rose was indeed late. In addition, Rachel said that when Jane got up to leave, she noticed that Rose seemed wobbly and smelled of alcohol. Rachel reported that Jane had said, "I am going to report you for being late and for coming to work intoxicated." Rose had already received a verbal warning for tardiness. According to Rachel, Rose then threatened Jane, saying, "You are a bitch. I'll complain to my union representative, and we'll see if you can get away with this."'"

Experience Made Randy Wise

Poor Randy—he walked right into this one. The union guns were loaded before he even got to work. Now he had a very upset staff and a big problem sorting it all out. Could he have handled this problem in a different way? Yes.

Here is what Randy could have done that probably would have decompressed the problem:

- With all of the information and events unfolding just a few minutes after Randy arrived at work, he should have stopped and analyzed the symptoms, identified the predictive symptoms, and developed a cause-and-effect statement like the following:

> The chain of events suggested that something must have happened between Jane and Rose, which was reported to the HR director and to the union representative by one of my dispatchers. Jane Bruning's frustration and attitude were the predictive symptoms.

- Randy should *not* have spoken to Rose and her union representative before getting all of the facts in the situation. The best bet would have been to contact the HR director first to get the lay of the land and then talk to others until he had all of the facts.

The story ended with Randy supporting Jane, Rose keeping her job but receiving a written warning, and many unhappy fellow employees claiming management had showed favoritism.

Grasping the Situation after the Fact

In my opinion, Randy failed and thereby paid the price of causing many unhappy employees and a poor reflection on his management skills. However, I did learn some good lessons from this story:

- When the symptoms of a problem start to hit you, slow down and do not take immediate action. Most of us can sense when something is different.
- Stop, look, and listen. Then gather all of the facts (symptoms). Then try to figure out what is going on. Then test your hypothesis. Then design action steps to fix the problem.

With one year to go until graduation, I was working on my dissertation (Staffing Practices and Life Style) when I decided it was time to get back to work so that my wife and family could settle down and get on with their lives. I was at a decision point: do I go back into the private sector or take up teaching as my work preference? Actually, this was a fairly easy decision to make. I had had enough of the company work environment and decided to turn to full-time teaching. I had been teaching a class at night at a local community college, and I found it challenging, which helped to swing my vote for academia.

I had no difficulty finding a position at a well-known state university where I was hired as the director of the Management Center in the College of Business Administration. With the faculty rank of assistant professor (the bottom rung on the academic ladder), I began with a salary many thousands of dollars less than I had been making in my last full-time, private-sector employment. So we packed up our family, sold our house, and headed to a new life of teaching, hoping that I could influence the way students and organizations managed change.

Teaching What I Have Learned Phase III

Glenn H. Varney, PhD

Teaching What I Have Learned

*It is one thing to read and study about how
to change organizations—it's quite
another to teach it, not to mention apply it.*

—Glenn Varney

It's a good thing I had a slow entry into the academic world. I had the summer to visit the campus, meet faculty and administrative personnel, and generally get oriented to academics before I began teaching a course in organization behavior to young undergraduates in the business school. What a shock it was to realize that upper-class-level students expected reading, lectures, and tests. They had little to no idea of how organizational behavior theories and concepts were developed (study and research in organizations), much less how they were applied in real organizations.

For example, leadership has been extensively researched, and the way in which different leaders lead and their impact on worker performance has been described. We know that dictators get negative or poor performance from workers while participative leaders get positive performance. Their lack of basic knowledge was so disappointing to me that during my first semester, I began to feel like I was silently losing my understanding of the real world where I had spent almost twenty years of my career.

What saved me was that I was still working on my dissertation, which was being conducted in a large oil company based out of Cleveland. My PhD was grounded in the following teacher's learning model:

1   Read / Study
       ↓
2   Show / Tell
       ↓
3   Apply / Experience
       ↓
4   Test in practice / Cases

So, brave me, I started to apply this to teaching organization behavior. Reading and study was homework. Classes became labs, storytelling, and experiential learning events. Tests consisted of a project paper applying theories and concepts to real-life organizations of the student's choice. I still used multiple-choice questions on the midterm and on a short final, but the main part of the grade was based on the real-life projects. The approach showed real transfer of learning possibilities, and the students loved it. No surprise, the Management Center offered opportunities for students to do real fieldwork, which brought to life what they were learning and testing in class.

Eventually, within about one and a half years, the department head and other faculty members began to ask questions, and this gave birth to the idea of a complete revision of the undergraduate major of personnel management. The new major was called organization development (OD), and the courses were designed around managing change in organizations. One of the courses was Fieldwork, in which students had to complete a change project in a real organization to which they were assigned. For example, a class of students studied levels of student computer competency. Their results were great and eventually guided the university's computer programming. Students loved it, employers got some project work done at little to no cost to them, and we could actually measure the learning.

The undergraduate OD program went well and was welcomed by the younger faculty, one of whom happened to be the assistant dean of the College of Business and a good friend of the dean. Organization development was new, refreshing, and it showed promise for a graduate-level program. I was asked to design a new graduate degree program, the Master of Organization Development (MOD), which was approved by the State Board of Regents four years after I started to work at the university.

Things were moving well for me until one day something yanked me off of my feel-good platform and brought me back to the reality of how inept organizations go about changing what they do and how they do it. The following story reminded me of how important it is to grasp the situation—in order not to fail.

Story 5—Failing to Grasp the Situation Leads to Failure

This story takes place in a large university where courses in leadership and management are taught every semester, where the scientific process is applied every day in labs and research centers on campus. It may seem impossible, but in institutions of higher learning, there are inadequate administrators, faculty members, and researchers who are actually teaching the correct way to identify and implement change but who are practicing just the opposite. It is a major boondoggle.

This all started one autumn day. I headed down the hall

to my office and noticed maintenance personnel working in several of the faculty offices in our wing of the building. It appeared as though they were replacing burned out fluorescent lightbulbs. I hadn't been in my office more than ten minutes when one of the maintenance mechanics showed up in my doorway carrying a short stepladder. "I have to remove two of your four lightbulbs," he said.

"Who gave you those directions?" I asked. He explained that the vice president of operations had ordered half of all the lightbulbs in the faculty offices and classrooms be removed.

"Why on earth would he tell you to do that?" I demanded. "It's already dark as a cave in my office; I don't have any windows."

"Don't ask me," he said. "I've worked here for fourteen years, and I've learned to do what I'm told and not ask questions."

He pushed his way into my office and was beginning to set up the ladder when he realized that my desk was positioned dead-center under the light fixture. "Looks like I'll have to stand on your desk to get those bulbs out," he said.

I had papers spread all over my desk, so I pushed them into a pile, moved them to one side, and he hopped up onto the desk. He removed the light-diffusing shade, took out two of the four fluorescent tubes, replaced the shade, and then left with no further conversation. When I looked out of my door, I saw a dim hallway and a number of angry faculty members standing outside of their offices.

When I got to my classroom that morning, it was almost too dark to read the white board. The students were complaining and talking about boycotting classes.

The entire university was in an uproar. I strained to make it through the material I had to present, and all the while I could hear murmuring and rumblings coming from the students in my class. When the class ended, I returned to my office to look for a memo of explanation. There it was in my in box:

To All Faculty Members and Staff

Due to power and fuel shortages, all lighting in classrooms and offices will be reduced by 50%.
In hallways and open areas, lighting will be reduced by 75%.
In addition, heating and air-conditioning will be adjusted as follows:

- **During the heating season, temperatures will be reduced by 10 degrees**

- **During air-conditioning season, temperatures will be set at 80 degrees.**

These changes will become effective immediately.

Stanley Haygood
Vice President of Operations

My research revealed that a five-member committee made up of the vice president of operations (PhD in economics), the director of maintenance (high school diploma), the operations engineer (MS in civil engineering), the chief personnel officer (BS in human resources), and the dean of student affairs (PhD in sociology) had been working for several weeks on a plan designed to reduce the university's energy usage by 25 to 30 percent. The plan was inspired by a federal mandate to reduce energy consumption, which in turn was being driven by a national fuel shortage. The university saw this as a perfect opportunity to reduce energy costs by as much as $750,000 per year at a time when the budget was very tight. Considered in that light, the actions being taken seemed to make some sense. Ah, but the story doesn't end there.

You would probably agree that students and faculty members tend to be rather bright and creative. Almost immediately, the faculty members brought in personal desk lamps to improve the lighting in their offices. Most of these had incandescent lightbulbs instead of fluorescent tube lights. They also brought free-standing, plug-in lighting for their classrooms. In the winter, they used electric space heaters, and in the summer months oscillating fans to cool their personal spaces. The students did the same in their dormitory rooms and in the common areas where they gathered to study and socialize.

Naturally, the university's electricity bill did not go down as expected by the mandate.

This activity continued for about a year, and then one day a terse announcement appeared on the campus hotline. It read:

> **All Light and Power Will Be Restored Immediately.**
> **Stanley Haygood**
> **Vice President of Operations**

So what was the net effect of this failure to grasp the situation? The university experienced an energy cost *increase* of almost $500,000 for the year in question.

Glenn H. Varney, PhD

The Rest of the Story

In most organizations, a person responsible for a $500,000 blunder would have been fired or at least demoted. That doesn't often happen in academia. Aside from the financial loss, it took years to restore the confidence of students and administrative staff to the point where they finally began to believe that the university's administrators had learned some lessons about how to manage change.

The VP of operations, Stanley Haygood, was slow to understand what had happened, but he had enough insight and openness to conduct a review of the costly blunder. He had served as VP of operations for ten years and during that time had become acquainted with many bright and capable individuals in the faculty and in administrative positions. He had a particularly close relationship with the provost of the university. I had gained a reputation on campus as a person of fairness, understanding, and caring when it came to introducing changes in relationships with faculty and support staff. The provost always engaged and consulted with students, faculty, and administrative staff before any actions and/or changes were made.

After the trauma from the painful lesson, Stanley asked to meet with me to discuss where he had gone wrong. I explained that there are three lessons you can learn from a failed change experience:

1. Always study and analyze the organization's culture so you will be able to predict how people will react to different strategies for change. Stanley might have asked others about making changes to the

physical plant in previous years and what reactions had been generated.

2. Be sure you engage all the stakeholders in designing and implementing change. Stanley might have explained the energy mandate and asked for input from all involved on how to implement the mandates.

3. Never forget that once you have activated a change strategy, continue the process to its conclusion. Stopping will usually only make things worse. Stanley might have modified the energy usage changes, explained them via e-mail or memo, then continued with some cost-cutting measures.

Grasping the Situation after the Fact

What a perfect learning experience for Stanley. He was lucky the university didn't sack him. However, he did seem to benefit from the experience, as his future change efforts *usually* called for a preliminary scan of the situation before he designed a change intervention. But he didn't always follow the advice of his data because he still had the attitude that he already knew the problem, and therefore his solution would work.

So what did I learn?

- Sometimes it takes a real shock to get a person to change. Part of grasping the situation is disposing of preconceived notions and having an open mind to reality.

- If you just ask people how they feel about a change, they will tell you what their reaction is or will be.
- Involving those affected in making change that they can live with almost always gets you buy-in for change.

Don't Become Overconfident

My next short story occurred about six years after I started to work with the university. By this time, I was feeling pretty confident and was sure I had a handle on change, particularly understanding and grasping the situation. Wrong! I really screwed up when I met Harold the Horrible.

Working with a good friend of mine, we helped destroy a leader and undermine an entire organization, all because we did not grasp the situation before we started the project.

Story 6—Harold the Horrible

This is not an ordinary story about change; it's more like a horror story. There is a tyrant who rules over his domain, villagers who labor under the control of the tyrant, a kindly king who doesn't understand what is happening, and a good wizard and his apprentice who come to liberate the king's subjects. Unfortunately, the story doesn't end with everyone living happily ever after. It is hard to believe that anyone could practice leadership the way this vice president did, ruling over his employees like a despot.

As you read this story, ask yourself if there is anything that would have signaled (predictive symptoms) the outcome.

_____

One bright summer afternoon, I returned from jogging in my neighborhood and heard the telephone ringing. As calls often meant a consulting opportunity, I hurried to answer it. When I answered, a man introduced himself as Jim King. "Do you remember me?"

I racked my brain trying to place the name, but it didn't immediately ring a bell. "The name is familiar, but I can't quite place you. Where did we meet?"

"At an Academy of Management conference in Dallas, Texas. I attended one of your presentations at the conference, and I'm very interested in your experiences in science-based change. I've just taken a job with a large stockbrokerage firm in New York City as their change agent."

His position, as he described it, was to help the organization improve its operations to become more humanistic by "cleaning up some of the bad parts of the organization."

Jim told me that he had called because of my reference at the conference to the field of organization development. He wanted my help in carrying out some change initiatives in his new company. He said he thought I might be of assistance to him in transforming some of the more difficult branch offices in the organization. He had one particular branch office in mind, located in Cleveland, Ohio, that needed immediate attention, and he asked if I would be interested in coming to his office in New York City to talk about it. I explained that I was going to New York City the following week to work with another client and could meet with him after those activities had concluded.

The following Thursday, I met with Jim at his

headquarters office in the financial district (not ground zero). I arrived about eleven thirty, and we had a brief introduction and reacquaintance. As we began talking about the problem branch, Jim suggested that we take the tour of his offices on the way out to lunch and that we talk in more detail at the restaurant.

He began to describe the situation in the Cleveland office, which was one of the company's largest branch offices, with over one hundred staff members, mostly brokers. He discussed the problems in terms of the vice president and said that the VP was a dominating person who had brought the organization to the point of uprising. Jim then pointed out that the branch was one of the highest performing offices in the organization (which seemed to me to be a contradiction). In addition, he reported that staff members in the branch office were expressing concern about a performance drop, but the vice president of the office had not reported anything of the kind.

I will refer to the branch office VP as Harold Despot. Jim asked if I would be willing to go out to Cleveland and sit down with Mr. Despot to see if I could help him improve his style of leadership. "You determine what has to change," Jim said, "and I'll make it happen."

I told Jim that while I would be interested in taking a stab at it, I did not want to do this one solo and would like to bring a good friend of mine, Ted Magek, into the process. Ted is a clinical psychologist and is an expert in dealing with leadership issues. I believed he would be very helpful in the situation Jim was describing.

Before we ended our conversation, I asked Jim to call Harold Despot and explain to him that we would be contacting him to set up a time to come in for a preliminary visit. Jim promised that if Mr. Despot resisted in any way he would let me know so that we would be aware of this when we called him to establish a meeting time. I hoped our first discussion with Harold Despot would give us a general idea of what the problem might be. Ted and I discussed the matter, and we estimated that the first visit would take no longer than two or three hours.

About a week after I returned from New York, not having heard anything to the contrary from Jim, I telephoned Harold Despot, and the receptionist answered the phone. She transferred me to Mr. Despot's secretary who said, in a bold and demanding voice, "Who are you and what is the purpose of your call?" She asked me to wait on the line and said that she would get back to me in a few minutes. It actually took her almost ten minutes to return to the line and then she reported that she had spoken to Mr. Despot, who wanted background information on me before he would agree to speak with me.

I referred to Jim King's call to Harold Despot, and I told her that I was calling at Jim's direction. Again she put me on hold and went back to speak with Mr. Despot. When she returned to the line, she said, "Mr. Despot is willing to meet with you on Monday, for about an hour, starting promptly at 9:00 a.m." I checked my calendar, and as it was already Thursday, that didn't give us much time to prepare, but I agreed to the date and time he had suggested.

On Monday, Ted and I arrived at the Cleveland, Ohio, office at 8:45 a.m. As we walked into the office, I noticed that it looked bleak and barren compared with the offices in New York. The receptionist was seated behind a glass panel, with a sliding window that was closed. She slid the window open and asked what we wanted. We explained that we had a meeting with Harold Despot at nine o'clock. She buzzed his secretary, and we were told that Mr. Despot would be with us shortly. At nine thirty, he came out of his office and shouted to his secretary so that everyone in the reception area could hear him, "Hey everyone! My shrinks are here!" We followed him through his secretary's outer office and into his office, where he sat down behind a very large mahogany desk and directed us to chairs in front of his desk. He was a commanding figure, about six foot three and weighing at least 250 pounds.

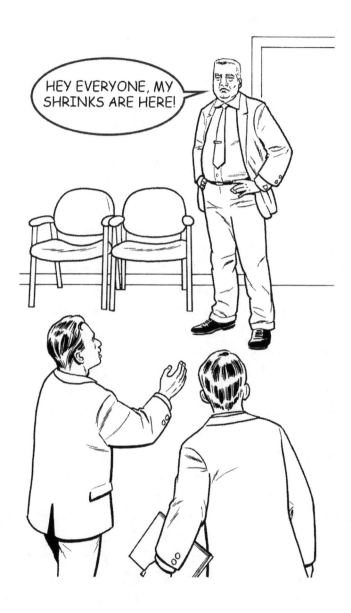

He sat in a plush leather chair while we sat in chairs at a slightly lower level. His first words to us were, "You can call me Mr. Harold Despot. Just who the hell are you guys? I have had a conversation with Jim King. In my opinion, he is a do-gooder who was hired to reform the organization to make it more lovable." He went on to say, "I suppose you have been hired to make me a more lovable person. It's all a bunch of nonsense, and I don't see the need for this sort of thing, but since the organization is willing to pay the bill, I simply can't turn away a freebie."

He wanted to know about our backgrounds, and he listened attentively as we told him about our experiences; this kind of surprised us. We asked him for a tour of his operation before we left, and he agreed. We also explained that we needed to get a better sense of what he and the other members of his immediate staff believed we should be looking for as we entered the organization.

We explained that gathering this information would involve interviewing some of his people and a further interview with him to enable us to develop a better understanding of how his organization functioned. We described in more detail that our next step would be to collect specific information about the organization from his staff. As there were more than a hundred staff members in the organization, we assured him that we would not be talking to all of his associates. After the interviews, we would analyze the data collected, summarize it, and place it in a presentable form so that we could have a feedback meeting with him and his immediate staff. This would give them all input into developing ways to deal with the various issues that were raised. This would identify issues/problems that he and his staff could collectively address.

We further explained that we had had some experience in working with client organizations that did not have a serious interest in taking the data and making action plans to improve the organization's performance. We told him that in retrospect, it had been a waste of their time and ours.

He replied, "That's not a problem here." We went over the confidentiality issue and told him that we would be careful to assure that the information that we gained from interviews and written surveys was kept confidential so that individuals would feel free to speak openly with us. Should we be asked to identify the individuals from whom we gathered specific comments or information, we would have to refuse.

He said, "I understand, and that makes good sense to me." He went on to say, "There are certain individuals in my organization who are troublemakers and/or bottlenecks. I want you to get the goods on them." We suspected that in the final feedback session he would try to pry information from us to identify specific individuals.

We explained that we could not be limited only to the items that he wanted us to look at but that instead we would strive to get at the issues troubling the members of his staff. We felt it was important to make this point to him, because we anticipated the possibility that he was not interested in hearing about his personal style of management. After all, it was his leadership style that had prompted Jim King to contact us in the first place. "You have nothing to worry about," Mr. Despot assured us. "Everything is working fine in my office." He said that he understood that the information we gathered would help the organization improve, and that improvement was his goal as well. At the end of the meeting, we suggested that we contact him to set up a follow-up visit, and he agreed.

Following our brief introductory meeting, he took us on a quick tour of the branch office. We walked out of his office into the area where his staff members and clerical associates were located. He announced to his secretary that he was "taking his shrinks on a tour." We cringed every time he referred to us as shrinks.

Our first stop was the area he called the boardroom, a large, open area with computers, desks, and people bustling about completing various tasks. It was arranged so that people sat at workstations facing the front of the room. Each desk had a computer on it with a broker assigned to that station. We entered the room from the rear so that all the individuals had their backs to us.

Harold Despot made no attempt to introduce us or to explain our presence in their midst. People were busy reading, talking on the telephone, and using their computers. One individual was standing in the middle aisle, reading what looked like the *Wall Street Journal.*

Mr. Despot reached down, took off his shoe, and shouted at the man, "Bill, wake up!" Then he threw the shoe at the man's paper, knocking it from his hands. The associate, who had nearly been hit in the face, turned around with an angry look and then quickly sat down at his desk. Harold Despot said, "Get the hell back to work."

As we moved through the office area, the brokers would turn around to glance at us and then promptly go back to what they had been doing. As we finished our quickie tour and walked out of the boardroom, a lone broker, looking a bit tattered, was entering the room. He wore a rumpled shirt, his tie was hanging loose, and he was not wearing a jacket. He seemed to be in a hurry. As he passed us, Harold Despot grabbed him by the arm and jerked him to a stop. He put the heel of his shoe on the toe of the associate's shoe and began grinding his heel into the broker's shoe. Harold Despot said, "Damn it, Ray, how many times do I need to tell you to polish your shoes." We were shocked and embarrassed to say the least.

When we returned to Mr. Despot's office, we discussed setting up a time for our meeting with his staff. He said he would make sure that everyone knew when and why we were coming and that he would have three of his top managers ready for us. We set the time and date, and then we left—glad to be escaping that environment.

As we were walking out of the office building, we passed a coffee shop and decided to stop, get a cup of coffee, and discuss the hour we had spent with Harold. I remarked, "I am astonished at the completely unacceptable behavior of a person who holds the position of vice president in a prestigious firm. His employees must be terrified of him and what outlandish thing he will do next." We were so shaken by our experience that we discussed ending our involvement immediately.

Ted said, "I'm afraid that the information we find will be so completely contrary to Harold Despot's self-image that he will reject it all out of hand." We predicted that this would create a major problem for his staff as well as for us. Ted continued, "I think Mr. Despot is in deep psychological trouble, and he might even be suffering from some type of mental disarrangement."

We were in agreement that Harold Despot seemed to

be domineering, controlling, and autocratic. He appeared to us to be out of control and perhaps even dangerous, but we were intrigued with the challenge of this project. After discussing it for some time, we decided to continue despite the potential hazards. Ted promised that he would stick with me to help navigate through the problems of dealing with Harold Despot.

Our next step was to call Mr. Despot to outline our intention of meeting for about an hour with each of his staff members as well as with him on the date he had set. He wasn't available to take our call, so we left a message with his secretary. We explained that we would be looking for a general sense of what the organization was feeling and trying to identify areas for improvement. We sought to assure him that we would not be focusing exclusively on him. We hypothesized that the reason this particular office was high performing was that Harold Despot was driving his employees to produce, with a whip and a chair! However, our experience told us that high performance levels could not continue in such an environment and that it was close to the breaking point, at which time performance would surely begin to decline. The focus of our study was to examine his staff's relationships, operating effectiveness, the physical layout and equipment, interpersonal relations, and Harold Despot's leadership style. The design seemed sound, and we planned a good organization development process. At least we thought it was good at that time.

Two weeks later, we returned to the office in Cleveland as scheduled. This time Harold Despot greeted us by proclaiming in a voice designed to carry through the entire building, "Well, my shrinks are back again." With that, we were off to a rocky start. We suspected that Mr. Despot had taken steps to assure that we would not be successful in gathering the needed information. We asked him to please not refer to us as shrinks, and his response was, "Why not? Aren't you shrinks? Do you dislike being called shrinks because that's what you are?" We tried to explain that using that term would cast us in a bad light and make it difficult for us to gather useful information. He scoffed at the idea, but he finally agreed to stop.

Next we interviewed Harold Despot. He gave us many insights into his view of the problems. "We need new computers," he said, "and my people don't put in eight-hour days. They spend their time loitering, staff members are not willing to stay over when needed, brokers don't make required client visits, and there are a number of other problems that a complete change of staff would solve." Although it seemed pointless, we asked him if he was interested in learning any information we might gather about his leadership style. "Don't waste your time on that stuff," he said. "I don't have anything to learn about myself; I know who I am. Focus on my staff, and it would be nice if you could get my staff members to give information about my immediate reports. And I certainly expect you to tell me what you learn about the behaviors of others that are causing disruption in my organization so that I can deal with it." This seemed to us to be more of a threat than a request for information.

Next we began talking to other members of his immediate staff. We followed the same line of questions that we had used with him. If you divide the one-hour interviews into parts, each staff member spent about forty-five minutes talking about the problems they had with Harold Despot. The problems they noted were numerous and frequently took the form of painful and vengeful complaints about him. "He is rude and hateful," they reported. "He thinks he is God on earth and we are here only to serve his needs. He has no consideration for others, and he makes demands that are impossible to meet. He loves to criticize us in front of the entire staff."

When we had completed the last of the interviews, we stopped in Harold Despot's office to let him know that we were leaving. He asked how the interviews had gone and what we had learned. We explained that we were not yet prepared to give any information because we hadn't had the chance to organize the data into a useful form or analyze it. "Oh well," he said. "I will get it eventually."

We took the information home with us to begin summarizing and formatting it in order to highlight details regarding his leadership and the other issues the staff members had raised. We developed a brief survey questionnaire that we planned to use with a group of staff brokers. In addition, we developed a second survey using the same types of questions, which was to be completed by the support/clerical group.

Ten days later, we returned to the Cleveland branch office and spent the day talking briefly to the brokers, and we also spoke with four or five members of the clerical group. We distributed the questionnaires and asked people to complete them on the spot. We explained the objectives of the project in general terms and found that many of the associates were not interested in participating for fear of being reprimanded by Mr. Despot. They said that they would be willing to complete the surveys and speak with us only if we could guarantee that they would not be identified. We assured them that our report would be a summarization, without identifying any of the participants, and would be shared not only with Harold Despot but also with all members of the organization.

The data were pooled and summarized so as to maintain privacy. About 70 percent of the employee responses were negative. In describing Mr. Despot, they used words such as *rude, domineering, mean, threatening,* and *abusive.* From our perspective, this was a devastating indictment of Harold Despot's leadership style. Ted said that in all his experience he had never seen anything like this. The harshness and negativity of the data presented us with a major challenge. How, we wondered, were we supposed to compile the information so that it would be helpful to the organization and not destructive? We had already committed to feeding back the information to Mr. Despot and to his entire organization. Because the data was high-impact, burning-platform information, we initially decided that our best chance of helping Harold Despot take the information seriously and motivating him to change lay in presenting the data to him and to his staff at the same time. However, Ted and I were worried that the data might be too powerful and that as we presented it, Harold Despot might react violently and stop the meeting. If that happened, nothing positive would be accomplished, and serious harm might be done. Instead we decided to meet with Mr. Despot to preview the results before the feedback session with the full staff. We prepared to present our findings to him with a great deal of trepidation.

The feedback session with the staff was scheduled for Saturday morning, so we met with Harold Despot late on Friday afternoon. He told us that although he did not have time to discuss the report with us then, he would read it and would call us at the hotel that night if he wanted to discuss it. We left the office worrying that he would read our report and destroy it, but we thought that he would probably still allow the feedback meeting to go forward.

We returned to the hotel planning to have dinner around six thirty. Just as I was changing to go out for dinner, Harold Despot called. He was furious! He began by screaming and calling me names. Then he said that he was coming over to the hotel to "straighten this out right now! No way," he said, "are you going to give this information to my staff. You stay right where you are! I'm on my way to the hotel."

I immediately called Ted to let him know what was going on. We agreed that we should meet down in the lobby so that there would be other people around which, we hoped, would cause Mr. Despot to keep his volume under control. Ted assured me that he would do what he could to calm the man down.

My phone rang, and Harold Despot said, "Get your ass down here right now." I met Ted at the elevator, and, taking deep breaths, we headed down to the lobby for our confrontation with Harold Despot. He met us in the bar, face flushed with anger. Throwing our report down on a bar table, he said, "Under no circumstances are you going to present this crap to my people tomorrow or any other time."

When we asked what he objected to, he said it was very simple. "You guys have made me out to be a tyrant." We tried to tell him that we had done nothing except report the words of his associates, but he said, "I don't give a damn what my people think. I'm not what they described, and you will not be presenting this stuff to my people tomorrow morning." All the while he was talking, he kept shaking his finger in my face, and he kept saying, "It is just not going to happen. This information won't help me or my organization." He said we were finished working for him and for his company, and he hissed, "When I get through, you won't be destroying any more organizations."

Harold the Horrible Does His Thing

We spent about an hour trying to calm him down but had little success. We cautioned him that if he went in tomorrow and told his people that the meeting was cancelled because he did not like the data, he would be confirming their complaints. We explained that his staff would know that he had put a stop to our efforts to improve the operation, and this would only make matters worse. He finally agreed to let us report the results to his staff, but he insisted, and he made us promise, that there would be no discussion following the presentation.

By the time he left, it was so late, and the meeting with Harold Despot had been so stressful, that Ted and I agreed to skip dinner, just get some sleep, and meet in the morning for breakfast to review what had occurred. The next morning, Ted and I met early and talked for almost two hours, reviewing the previous night's discussion and preparing for our meeting with the staff. We planned to cast the meeting in such a way that Harold Despot would not be able to accuse us of being the bad guys. We decided to explain at the start of the meeting that Mr. Despot had seen the information the night before and had already had a chance to comment on it.

The meeting was well attended, and as we presented the data, we highlighted the positive aspects first to put the best face possible on the material. However, when we got to the negative aspects, Harold Despot openly said that he did not like the words his employees had used, and he was dissatisfied with a great portion of the report. As we continued presenting the data we had collected, you could see people cringe and withdraw. They were hunkering down, waiting for the explosion, and hoping the presentation would finish quickly. Harold Despot just sat there frowning, with his arms crossed, and he frequently left to get coffee. Each time he returned, he would stand at the back of the group and appear very agitated and irritated. At the end of the presentation, we intended to ask the group to validate the information to check its accuracy but not to discuss or expand on the data. However, as we finished reviewing the report, Harold Despot shouted, "That's it; we are now going back to work. We will discuss this at our next staff meeting when there are no shrinks present. This meeting is now ended." With that, the group made a rapid exit—it looked like a fire drill. Harold Despot grabbed my copy of the report, and without even acknowledging us, he stormed from the room. It wasn't hard to conclude that we were finished in his organization.

We were worried about how Harold Despot would react to his people once they were back in the organization, so on the first working day following the meeting, we called three of the key staffers to offer help in dealing with him. Their response was, "We are not allowed to talk to you now or in the future; we have been instructed not to work with you in any way."

We heard nothing more from Harold Despot or his company until three months later. Then I received a call from Jim King who asked, "What in the hell happened in Cleveland?" I told Jim that Harold Despot had refused to work with us to complete the project and that he had threatened to ensure that we did no more work with the company in the future. Jim asked for details about what had transpired. When I explained, he asked for a copy of the report. I suggested that he ask Harold Despot for a copy, and Jim replied, "He has refused to give me one." I expressed disbelief that one of his direct reports could refuse his request, but Jim King ignored my comment and simply said that he regretted the way the whole project had turned out. He commented, "Harold Despot needs a lot of help, and he's not getting it."

The Rest of the Story

About a year after our experience with this client, we learned that several months after our report meeting, Harold Despot's daughter was seriously injured in an auto accident, and he suffered a heart attack followed by a nervous breakdown. He remained on leave of absence for some time, and when he finally returned to the company, it was in a preretirement position of much lower responsibility. The company transferred someone new into the Cleveland branch office as vice president, and the operation was running somewhat better than it had been. This was a major learning experience for us, and the lessons Harold Despot taught me will forever echo in my mind.

Take a look at the clues/symptoms that gave us fair warning that the project was doomed to fail:

1. Before visiting the operation, Jim had said the following:
    a) "help Harold improve his leadership style"
    b) "problem office"
    c) "leader is a domineering person"
    d) "organization is at the point of uprising"
    e) "staff concerned about a performance drop, but vice president not reporting it"
2. During our first introductory meeting:

a) delays waiting to see Harold
b) outdated physical surroundings
c) "I'm waiting to see my shrinks."
d) office layout
e) "Call me Mr. Despot."
f) "Who the hell are you guys?"
g) "You are here to make me a more loveable person."
h) "It's all a bunch of nonsense; don't need this sort of thing."
i) "I'm taking my shrinks on a tour."
j) shoe-throwing incident
k) ground heel of his shoe on broker's shoe
l) "Get the hell back to work."

I still struggle with the question of why we took on this project in the first place. The best answers I have are that

- we felt sorry for Mr. Despot's staff and thought we might be able to help them, and
- if we could pull this off, we might get more work in other branches of the organization.

Grasping the Situation after the Fact

You would think that with all the experience I had I would have been able to see this one coming. So why was I so blind or why did I refuse to see, or ignore, the telltale signals Harold was sending? As I look back, three things stand out:

- I was impressed with myself and felt that Ted and I could handle this client situation. I was just plain overconfident, which blinded me to the clues that predicted failure.
- Money was driving a lot of things that motivated me. I wanted a new car, I was buying a second home, and so on. The money came first; client welfare was second or maybe even last.
- Perhaps the most damning, I thought I knew human behavior, but I didn't. I simply did not see Harold as the tyrant he was. I should have drawn a line and stopped when he began throwing shoes at his staff.

This project failed at the time because I did not grasp the magnitude of the situation. I rationalized my actions by convincing myself that it was likely that Harold would have collapsed on his own; all I did was speed up the process.

Sometimes the symptoms of a problem are right in front of you, and you can't recognize them for what they are. The next story is an example of how important it is to be alert for clues (symptoms) of a larger problem. When a symptom catches your attention, it can be like an early warning of an impending problem that needs your attention and fact-finding efforts—right now!

Story 7—Subtle Symptoms—Miss Them and Pay the Price

William Cummings, the CEO of a large manufacturing plant in Michigan, was having lunch with Tom Duncan, the mayor of the small town in which the plant was located. They were discussing how important the startup of a new factory would be to the economy of their community and what they could do to attract such a company to the area. Changing the subject, Mayor Duncan commented to Bill, "I hear you have a major problem with your union. According to the grapevine, your unionized employees are very unhappy with their union leadership."

"Really?" said Bill. "I hadn't heard that, but I will most certainly look into it."

The Mayor's Surprise

As soon as lunch was over, Bill returned to his office and called a meeting with his production manager,

Bob Strong, and his human resources manager, John Cervantes. He began the meeting by asking how things were going on the floor and what they were hearing from the workforce.

"Everything is running smoothly," said Bob. "The Ferguson order will be completed ahead of schedule and with less overtime than we had projected."

"That's good," said Bill. "And how about your area, John? How are the folks on the floor feeling?"

"I spoke with the union president this morning," John replied, "and he said that aside from a few grievances about wearing safety glasses in the canteen area, everyone seems happy, particularly with the latest round of wage increases."

"Then why," demanded Bill, "did the mayor tell me at lunch that our unionized employees are very unhappy with their leadership?"

Bob and John just stared blankly at each other. Finally John said, "He must be thinking of some other company. No one here has said anything about our associates having problems with their union."

"Well, he didn't seem confused to me," said Bill. "I sure hope there's nothing hiding in the weeds that you two have missed."

"He probably just heard a few employees grumbling about our new production standards," said Bob.

"If Bob says so, it must be true," John agreed.

Before the month was out, several employees were circulating a petition to have their local union removed and replaced with a union more to their liking. Apparently, a lot of employees were dissatisfied with the current union leadership—71 percent of the unionized workforce signed the petition! Within six months, the union that had represented the employees for years was gone and had been replaced by the much more aggressive Factory Workers International Union. Bill found himself in negotiations for a new union agreement with professional union representatives who demanded significantly higher wages and benefits, and new production standards that would reduce output and increase overtime opportunities.

It should come as no surprise that Bill was soon advertising for a production manager and a human resources manager. The advertisements listed "significant experience in unionized environments" as a must-have for all who wished to apply.

The Rest of the Story

Although it was already too late by the time Bill heard about the union petition being circulated, he immediately started to dig into the problem. He discovered that there had been many symptoms of the problem as it was developing that never found their way to his attention. For example:

- Bob Strong, the production manager, had been changing production standards without informing or seeking agreement with the union.
- John Cervantes, the HR manager, was instructed by Bob Strong, "Stay away from the union, and if necessary, stay out of the plant until the standards installation is completed."
- The salaried lead supervisor had been promoted from the hourly (union) ranks and withheld

information about employee discontent with the union.

- Because the plant was in a small, closely knit community, the word spread rapidly to people like the mayor, who had family members working in the plant.

There were few visible signs/symptoms of the coming union problems because communication and flow of information were being blocked, filtered, or changed primarily by Bob, John, and the lead supervisor.

Bill should have followed up on the trigger comments made by Mayor Duncan ("I hear you have a major problem with your union. According to the grapevine, your unionized employees are very unhappy with their union leadership."). Instead of asking the mayor for more details, Bill chose to look into it back at the plant.

Bill also missed a very obvious symptom—John's statement, "If Bob says so, it must be true." This comment should have been enough to galvanize Bill into investigating the relationship between his production manager and his human resources manager. He could have started with John in a one-on-one meeting to find out why and what he was holding back.

These mistakes turned out to be very costly for Bill, who found himself wrestling with a new union demanding changes in the production standards and increases in wage rates. This in turn led to a decrease in productivity, increased costs, and a very unhappy corporate headquarters. You can be sure that Bill never made this mistake again.

A Sidebar on Symptoms

Multiple events and situations occur every day that influence our work environments and even the very lives of our organizations. Many times these events go unnoticed, or, if they are noticed, they are considered unrelated bits and pieces. However, when taken together, these events can have meaning that signals the need for attention and change.

Health is a good example. We all experience physical discomforts. Often we simply attribute them to something we ate, or old age, or phantom pain. We say to ourselves, "I'll just wait a bit and see if it goes away." Only if the discomfort is persistent and inhibiting do we pay attention to it. We might finally reach the point where we recognize a particular discomfort as a symptom of something that has changed for the worse. This is when most of us reach for the telephone to call the doctor. We expect the doctor to analyze our symptoms, diagnose the problem, and prescribe something to make it better.

The same holds true in our organizations. Every day, things occur that are out of the ordinary. It could be something as simple as a few people being a little late for work, or a piece of production equipment that begins making a strange squeaking sound. Perhaps a coworker who is usually cheerful and outgoing suddenly becomes grumpy or standoffish. These little things, disorders if you will, seem small at the time, but if they are ignored, they can lead to larger problems like missed deadlines, the loss of an important customer, or the resignation of a key employee.

The point is that we all need to be more sensitive

and aware of changes in our organizations. We should recognize that small problems can grow into big problems and address them before they become issues that are more difficult to resolve and more resistant to correction. Looking for these little indicator symptoms and becoming more sensitive to the surroundings so that symptoms can be identified early are essential skills for leaders and change agents.

Symptoms of problems are not always internal. Many times the origin and cause of a symptom can be traced from outside the organization back to its source. In this story, the trigger symptom appeared outside the organization.

Grasping the Situation after the Fact

In the case of Bill and the union problem, failure actually led to success. I was working as a consultant to Bill in this matter, and the union problem put us on alert for more symptoms of problems in the organization.

It is very tempting to wander off and point the finger of blame when in reality this is as simple as paying attention to your inner voice that is telling you that something isn't right. The CEO had an inner sense that there was something wrong in his organization when Bob and John both had blank looks on their faces while Bill reported what the mayor had told him about union unrest.

There are three points of learning from this experience that will make you wise:

- When you sense a problem, track it down. Don't wait to let it erupt into an event.

- Put in place sensing posts that will signal potential problems.
- Ignore the symptoms of a brewing problem at your own peril.

A Turning Point in My Learning about Change
Phase IV

Glenn H. Varney, PhD

A Turning Point in My Learning about Change

Looking back at failed/flawed projects was an eye opener. Then Scott Janoch came along.

Before I proceed, I need to describe what my approach to change consulting was at this time. I had developed presentations, lectures, and training programs that got rave reviews for delivery and content. Audiences loved the humor, wit, and stories I told about how effective what I was teaching was in changing the way people worked.

I wrote a book on goal and objective setting for leaders, and I went around the United States and Europe telling everyone that what I was teaching would make them great leaders. It never occurred to me that the members of my audiences could not apply what I was talking about. Their organizations just were not ready to apply what I was teaching, and, in fact, many of the people attending my lectures were there simply to get out of the office and take a break. What was the point of making a presentation to a group of people if it just went in one ear and out the other? What I was doing was pitching an intervention that in 90 percent of the cases wouldn't work. I was putting the cart before the horse, proposing an intervention with no idea of whether it would or could work, much less improve performance as I was advocating.

With this realization, I decided to take a look at the way I had been approaching change. This in turn led to a self-evaluation and began my conversion to a diagnostic or evidence-based approach to change. In short, I realized that if I wanted to improve my batting average (reduce failures), I needed to understand the problem I was trying to correct before I began designing a solution (intervention). I was beginning a transformation that might be described thusly:

- First, training is an intervention designed to change something or someone. Without understanding the problem/condition that needs to be changed, the result is trying to teach people something they cannot put into their work lives, and it does little or nothing to improve performance.
- Second, developing a fancy, new flavor-of-the-month program may make you some money, but it does little to change people, much less organizations. Besides, you'll just have to come up with a new flavor when they get tired of the old one. I had already experienced this phenomenon.
- Third, most of what I was doing was prescribing solutions without understanding the problem I was trying to solve. If I had gone to a physician with a complaint, and he had prescribed a treatment procedure without performing a thorough diagnostic process, I would have quickly found another doctor. I think some of my clients did just that.
- Fourth, I had painfully learned a number of lessons.
  - o Always learn about your client (who, what, when, why, and how).
  - o Before you agree to take on the project, conduct a preliminary scan.
  - o Strong leaders, not browbeaters but leaders who inspire and lead by example, have a lot to do with successful change. They understand that what's good for the goose is good for the gander.

- o Understanding the culture of the organization is essential if you want to help people change. There are many theories and behavior concepts that will be of help to you as you work to help people and organizations change.
- o Symptoms of the problem begin to show up well in advance of the manifestation of the problem itself. Be alert to the early warning signs. Don't wait for the explosion—ignore the early symptoms of a developing problem at your own peril.
- o Always engage the people you are seeking to change. If you do, they will work with you.
- o Overconfidence leads to failure. Never take on a project unless you are *sure* you can help.
- o Remember to view the overall picture and not just a single symptom.

My learning to date caused me to reassess the way in which I approached a client problem. After some deep thinking, I diagrammed my new approach to change projects as follows:

1

Identify the pain. Why does the client want your help? →

2

Perform a preliminary scan. Identify and list symptoms.

↓

3

Put the pieces together. What are the causes and effects?

↓

7

Measure the results of your intervention to make sure it works.

↑

4

Test your conclusions. How do you know you're right?

↓

6

Design and test an intervention. How do you know it will work? ←

5

Validate the results of your cause-and-effect test. Does the client agree with your diagnosis?

Example:

1	→	2
The VP of a television station reports that his CEO blocks all new ideas.		Talk with the VP of the facility and meet with others who have the same complaint.

↓

3

Heard that the CEO scoffed at and rejected all new ideas.

↓

7

Checked later with the VP, and he reported great improvement.

4

Checked and confirmed that this was the case.

↓

↑

6	←	5
Met with the CEO and role-played his behavior. It was an eye-opener for him, and he agreed to change.		Reported back to the VP for confirmation that I had it straight.

It was at this point in my change management development that Scott Janoch entered my life. I met Scott in 1992 when a close friend asked me to help him with union contract negotiations in one of his company's manufacturing plants. The union and management were at each other's throats, and agreement seemed impossible. He described the situation as impending war and wanted to see if there was a nontraditional approach that might bring the parties to agreement.

This was a large, foreign-owned company of which my friend was the vice president of human resources, and Scott Janoch was the company's director of labor relations. Scott had a large stake in the issue and in what his boss was asking me to do. He was as skilled and experienced in labor relations and contract negotiations as anyone I had ever met, and in no uncertain terms he challenged my approach. However, he agreed to keep an open mind and to work with me in trying to change the entire work environment and relationship with the union in the troubled plant. From this experience, Scott and I formed a lasting friendship and work partnership that continues to this day. Here's the story of our first change project working together.

Story 8—"Blah! Blah! Blah! You're Fired."

For this project, I consciously tried to apply what I had learned from previous projects. It turned out that Scott and I did a great job of beginning a change process that should have been a first-class success story. However, to our bewilderment, the Italian owners of the organization decided to cancel the project. When we asked why it was being cancelled, the only words the operations vice president could speak in English were, "Blah, blah, blah, you're fired." Read the following story carefully and see if you can spot a clue as to why this change project failed.

I was in New Jersey doing some consulting work for Clark Campbell, an old friend of mine. He was the North American vice president of human resources for AJX Incorporated, a multinational corporation headquartered in Milan, Italy. The company produced everything from telecommunications products to automobile tires. As North American VP, Clark was responsible for nine different manufacturing facilities that were located in the United States and Canada. When we took a break from our discussion, Clark began describing the troubles that were plaguing one plant in particular, the AJX plant in Bluffton, California, a telecommunications plant that produced miles and miles of cables each year.

"For a plant that specializes in communications products, Glenn, we sure have problems talking to our employees," said Clark. I nodded, and Clark rubbed his forehead waiting for me to comment. When I didn't, he continued.

"The union in Bluffton is all up in arms right now; the situation is the worst it has ever been. Their contract is about to expire, and we've been going back and forth on health care. The health care costs of that plant have gone through the roof since the last contract, but the union workers simply refuse to accept an increase in what they have to pay. However, that's just the tip of the iceberg. We have gone through nine plant managers in the past ten years—some have quit, and others have been terminated. There have been discussions about shutting the plant down permanently. No one is happy.

The workers say management will not listen to their concerns, and management thinks that catering to the workers' every whim will eventually bankrupt the place. Glenn, we've had some ugly negotiations in the past, but this one is shaping up to be war. If something doesn't happen soon, my instincts tell me those guys are going on strike." He shuffled the papers we had been working on, and then he sighed. "Sometimes I think the Italians just don't understand American business." He pulled out his handkerchief and cleaned the lenses of his glasses. "We've had some close calls in this plant in the past, but this time I would bet that in a matter of months the employees will be walking the picket line. The situation has all the makings of a disaster."

I took it all in and then asked, "Have you thought about approaching the problem in a different way?"

"I'm listening," Clark said. "What do you have in mind?"

"Well, let's try some new ideas. How about getting the workers involved in operating the plant?" I asked. "If the workers felt a sense of ownership in the plant, they might be less likely to make demands that can't be met." Clark jotted down a few notes and asked a few questions. When I had answered them, he looked at his watch and stood up. "How about some coffee before we get back to work?" he asked.

"Okay," I said. "Make mine black." I waited in Clark's office for what seemed like a very long time before he returned, without the coffee.

"He bought it," Clark said.

"Who bought what?" I asked. "What are you talking about?"

"The who," said Clark, "is John Cooper, the president

85

of North American operations and my boss. I told him about your ideas for Bluffton, and he wants to try it." I just looked at him in surprise. "John is planning to check into a few things, and he is going out to Bluffton soon to speak to the employees face-to-face, but the bottom line is he wants you to get the ball rolling out there."

"And I thought you were just going for coffee!" I exclaimed.

Following the president's visit to Bluffton, I took a trip out there myself. It was a dusty little town with a small strip of fast-food restaurants at one end and the AJX plant at the other. Railroad tracks skirted the west edge of the town, and beyond the tracks was a low desert, sparsely populated by a few scattered ranches. There couldn't have been more that three thousand people in the town, and aside from AJX, there was no other industry nearby.

Prior to my arrival, President Cooper had met with the employees concerning the idea of getting them involved in solving the plant's problems. He had offered the roughly one hundred unionized employees an eighteen-month extension of their current contract plus an extra thirty-five-cent-per-hour wage increase if they would agree to work with management to change and improve the plant operations. He also promised them that everyone would have input in the selection of the next plant manager. After deep deliberation, the union agreed to the plan. I came prepared to begin the process, and I brought with me a young graduate student named Brian.

Our first challenge came just a few days after our arrival. Brian and I were asked to address all of the employees about the change process we were trying to initiate. I explained our ideas for change to small groups of employees in the plant conference room, a stuffy place with overhead fans whipping up the dust. I stressed to everyone that I would be working for them as well as for AJX management and that I would be responsible to all of them. When I had finished, we polled each group to see if they wanted to proceed. Seventy percent of the employees agreed to begin the process, with the clear understanding that they could call a halt to the effort at any time.

Our game plan involved forming a team, comprised of both management and union employees, charged with the task of studying the possibilities of fundamentally changing the entire operation in Bluffton. We called this group the "change team," and their job was to distill ideas we wished to incorporate at AJX and then present them to the employees and to management. They would develop a vision statement and present that to the employees as well. Once a vision had been created and approved, more groups would be formed, including hourly and management employees, to make the vision a reality. The overall purpose was to get management and the employees working together for the common good of the plant, thus building relationships at the person-to-person level that would eventually translate into a stronger trust between employees and management.

We learned early on that trust was sorely lacking between these two groups. We began by asking for volunteers to join the change team. We did not want to let the AJX Union Executive Board (the E. Board) select the hourly change team members from the list of volunteers. This process irritated some of the union members who insisted that the E. Board should appoint the hourly team members and that union members of the change team should outnumber the management members. We struggled with these issues, but we eventually persuaded all employees that the consultants, not the E. Board, had designed the selection criteria for the team members and should make the selection based on these criteria. We explained that we wanted to keep the selection process as objective and nonpolitical as possible.

"If you want to blame someone for the selection criteria," I told the employees as we met with them, "blame us, the consultants. After all, we work for all of you just as much as we work for management." Once we got past that hurdle, we still had the major task of selecting the union members of the change team from among the forty-seven volunteers. The change team was to be composed of eleven members, five union employees, four salaried employees, the union president, and the plant manager. We wanted the union president and the plant manager on the team to show their involvement and support and to lend their authority to the process.

One member of the E. Board, a man named Simmons, had volunteered for the change team. He had the support of many of the union members, but he also had a reputation for being a hothead. He was a real Jekyll-and-Hyde sort whose temper could blow at the slightest provocation. He had even been involved in several fights on the floor of the plant. A tall man with broad shoulders and a drooping mustache, he had a habit of poking his finger into your chest when he talked with you and wanted to make a point. I believed that he had strong-armed his way into his union leadership position and would be a distraction and a hindrance if he were on the change team.

When we announced whom we had selected to be on the change team, Simmons was not included, and the E. Board members went bananas. They pushed back their chairs and stormed out of the room in a cursing rabble. We could see them through the windows, standing outside, swinging their fists in the air and pounding on the picnic tables in disgust. They kept this up for some time, but at last they came back inside and agreed that Simmons would not be on the change team. In a way, I think this small victory increased the trust of the employees in our objectivity.

The man we had chosen in place of Simmons was a slight, quiet man, George Beck. I would almost describe him as mousey. When he learned of his selection to the change team, his face lit up, and he said, "I've been waiting all my life for a chance like this." As it turned out, this quiet little man had some of the best ideas of anyone, and he proved that a man like Simmons, popular though he might be, is not always the most valuable contributor to a change process.

Once the change team had been formed, we set about educating the team members by presenting information about other plants that had gone through similar change processes. The idea was to allow the group to see the possibilities. Over the course of several months, the team made visits to plants in Columbus, Ohio; Bowling Green, Ohio; and, by far the most popular, the Harley-Davidson motorcycle plant in Milwaukee, Wisconsin. Members of the change team were able to see firsthand the successes and failures of similar change efforts. In addition, they completed weekly reports and presented them to their fellow employees at the plant, so that everyone was kept informed of their activities and progress.

As the weeks and months passed, workers who had been skeptical at first began to get behind the reorganization process. In September, the economy took a downturn, and a 25 percent drop in production made layoffs necessary. In order to demonstrate his commitment to the plant's future, President Cooper came to the plant in person to pledge that the change process would continue despite the decline in production. Something happened to Mr. Cooper while he was in the plant that reinforced his confidence in the eventual success of our efforts. He told me later that while he was walking the floor of the plant, one of the union employees stopped him. Even though this employee was scheduled to be laid off the following day, he insisted that the change process would be successful in Bluffton. He held Cooper's arm as he practically demanded that the process continue, and he spoke to him for some time about his enthusiasm and the excitement of other employees about the progress they could see developing. In fact, many workers who were being laid off asked that the change team's weekly progress reports be mailed to their homes so that they could keep up with developments. Of course, President Cooper agreed.

It was during this time that I began to realize just how much working for AJX meant to many of the employees. It was more than a job to them; it was their livelihoods, and they took great pride in their work. At our change team meetings, discussions often became heated. During a break one afternoon, I was standing by the door getting a breath of air. The union members of the team had the habit of standing around the picnic tables outside having a smoke, and one of the men broke away from the group and came toward me. I recognized him as Goddard, a Harley-Davidson buff who rode his motorcycle to work. He was a bear of a man, 270 pounds at least, with a massive stomach and chest. As he stood in front of me that afternoon, he towered over me, invading my personal space, and he made me uncomfortable. Pointing his finger at me, he said, "You guys are not going to tear this place down, not after we've worked so hard." He smoothed back his reddish hair and adjusted his ponytail before continuing. "This is our plant; this is our home. All that stuff on paper is fine, and maybe it works at other places. But this place is different." He edged even closer to me, and I could smell the stale tobacco odor on his breath and in his scraggly beard. He hitched up his pants by a belt loop and said in a voice that came from deep in his barrel chest, "All this talk is one thing, but we've got families to think of."

"I know," I quietly assured him. "This is going to work out. It just takes a while."

"Maybe we don't have a while," he said. Goddard then went on to tell me about his family, the monthly mortgage on his house by the railroad tracks, his father's illness, and other personal details. He talked about the town of Bluffton and how the population had been declining for years. He worried that AJX Corporation might be the only thing keeping the little town on the map. By the time he had finished speaking, Goddard had tears in his eyes. He wiped his nose and looked at me. I had no idea what to say to him, and still he didn't move.

Finally I said, "You made your point. You've said it so

well I can feel what you're going through. I can tell what this means to you."

Wiping the tears from his eyes, he said, "Yeah, well good. Don't screw this up!"

By November, the change team had hammered out a vision for the plant, despite animosity from some union leaders. The union president, George, and the vice president, Anderson, had arrived hours late for meetings on more than one occasion, claiming, "We didn't think this was an important meeting." It was their way of demonstrating their power and reminding people that they weren't just toothless company lapdogs. Despite their game playing, the vision statement came together, and the change team presented it in special meetings with small groups of workers. The vast majority of employees were impressed by the work the change team had done, and they voiced their support more than ever. When George and Anderson began to see the support their fellow employees were giving to the effort, they changed their tunes and got behind the process. By late November, we were running on all cylinders, and the attitude in the plant was enthusiastic, encouraging, and optimistic.

In early December, four design teams consisting of five to six members each were formed from a pool of hourly and management volunteers. All of those who volunteered were placed on one of these four teams. These teams were charged with producing a detailed plan that would then be proposed to all of the plant employees and to the company's North American management team. Weekly meetings were scheduled as forums for sharing ideas and collecting information. They also served as communication channels to all of the plant employees.

The change team remained operational as well in order to help facilitate discussion among the four design teams. To further involve plant employees, the design teams began to hold open meetings that anyone could attend, and all attendees were encouraged to voice their ideas and suggestions.

January saw a visit from a vice president from the AJX Italian corporate office, Mr. Vecchio. His English was poor, so he brought an interpreter with him. Clark Campbell came to Bluffton with them to give them a tour of the facility. Through the interpreter, Mr. Vecchio spoke with many of the employees. He was a solemn, intense man with dark, heavy eyebrows. He made copious notes in a small notebook that he carried in his breast pocket. The vision statement had been posted on the wall in the plant lobby just before Mr. Vecchio's arrival, and he studied it closely, making page after page of notes. When I asked Clark what had prompted the visit, he assured me that it was just routine and that the change process would continue as planned.

However, a few weeks later, a Frenchman by the name of Albert Lesheve arrived at the plant. He had been appointed by the corporate headquarters in Italy to be the new plant manager. As it happened, we were in the final stages of selecting a new plant manager from the available candidates. As part of his effort to get the employees to participate in the change process, President Cooper had promised them that they would be involved in selecting the next plant manager. It was part of the deal that had extended the union agreement and brought about the initiation of the change process. They had narrowed the field to several candidates that the plant employees had approved and were preparing to make an offer to one of them. The arrival of Albert Lesheve preempted the entire process.

Naturally, the employees were furious that the Italian headquarters had overridden their agreement with the North American operations president, and they insisted that Albert return to France. Their protests were ignored, and Albert stayed. You can imagine the position that put the new plant manager in and the impact this betrayal would have on the entire change process.

Albert's every decision was resisted. It was clear that the employees resented his very presence. His lack of support for the change process didn't win him any friends either. He quickly became aware that his authority carried almost no weight. One day he invited Brian and me to lunch to discuss the progress of the change process in Bluffton. Halfway through lunch, Albert put his fork down and in a casual but condescending tone said, "Dr. Varney, I want to inform you that your services are no longer needed."

"Albert," I replied matter-of-factly, "I don't think you have the authority to dismiss me."

He became disturbed and said, "You are not allowed to continue what you are doing. It is a failure, and you must go."

Brian and I looked at each other for a moment, and then, very calmly, I replied, "No one has told us this but you. The president of the North American operation, your boss as I understand it, hired us, and we are not leaving. The change process isn't stopping either."

Albert's face reddened, and he picked up his fork and resumed eating his lunch. He didn't say another word to us. However, this discussion was an indication of the problems that would eventually be the undoing of the change process at the Bluffton plant. Just a few short weeks later, our success would be discarded.

Just as the plant was preparing to implement the first of the changes that the design teams had developed, I received a call from my friend Clark. "Glenn," he said, "Milan headquarters just called me. They want to meet with you, me, and President Cooper in the next few days."

"What's up?" I asked.

"I don't know," said Clark. "Neither does Cooper. Or if he does, he isn't telling me. All I know is Milan representatives are flying in specifically for this meeting."

A few days later, we met at the division headquarters in Lexington, South Carolina, with a large, muscular Italian named Marko Boratino. He had brought with him an interpreter and a European consultant. President Cooper was not in attendance. I asked, "Why isn't Mr. Cooper here?" Marko Boratino just shrugged, but a few minutes later, Cooper arrived in the room. Cooper shook hands and then told us all good-bye. He explained that he had been terminated and was leaving immediately. This would be a definite blow to the change process in Bluffton, I thought. Cooper, the man who had authorized the process and given us the go ahead, had just been fired.

Still, Clark and I proceeded with our presentation to Mr. Boratino and his entourage. They seemed disinterested, not really paying attention to the process or its details. We outlined the entire project for them, from start to finish, detailing the results of the employee polls and describing the enthusiasm and commitment of the employees. The consultant appeared bored and distrustful. Finally, I presented a copy of the plant vision statement and laid it on the table. "Ninety-five percent of the Bluffton employees agree that this is the right thing to do for the operation," I said. "Eight months ago, the management and the union were at each other's throats. You were facing a long and bitter strike. Now we have support for a plan that nearly everyone accepts and is enthusiastic about. This is a major step in the right direction. You should accept and support this plan," I concluded.

When the interpreter had finished translating, Boratino sat in silence, picking his teeth. At almost the same time, Clark and I said, "We are ready to move forward with this; all we need is the approval to go ahead."

Boratino took the toothpick from his mouth, waved his hand dismissively, and then said, "Blah, blah, blah."

"What is that supposed to mean?" I asked the consultant and the interpreter.

"It means," replied the interpreter, "that he thinks all of this is nothing but a bunch of talk."

Clark interjected, "Our employees want and need this. Doesn't that mean anything to you?"

Boratino stood and began to leave the conference room. Just before he reached the door, he turned and, in perfect English, said, "You will stop this now!"

The Italian Owners Pull the Plug

I kept thinking of all the hard work the employees in Bluffton had put into this effort, every step of the way. I thought of Goddard, seeing the tears on his face as he described what the operation meant to him and to the entire community. I wished he had been there, and I felt compelled to speak for him and for all of the plant employees. "You can't do this," I said. "You're making a big mistake. This isn't Italy!"

"No one threatens me," said Boratino, again in perfect English, as he walked from the room. He made the statement flatly, without passion, and I understood clearly that we had been dismissed. I left to return home.

Clark was terminated soon after that, but when the smoke had cleared, he was asked by the Italian management to return to AJX. He refused. Through Clark, I later learned that when the negotiations began with the union, some nine months later, the employees went on strike. The company threatened to permanently close the plant, and the union gave in and returned to work after one week. Bitter wounds that had begun to heal were reopened between the management and the employees in Bluffton. The situation eventually resulted in the failure and closing of the operation.

Grasping the Situation after the Fact

When you think you have learned a lesson, sometimes you find you are still in the learning process.

This situation did not end with the closing of the Bluffton, California, plant. Other plants were also closed, and eventually the North American company was sold. Tragically, the new owners continued the same old-fashioned, aggressive approach to the union-represented plants, leaving hundreds of good people out of work as a result of continuing labor difficulty and numerous plant closings.

From the viewpoint of the consultants, this whole project was a sweet and sour experience. On the one hand, the relationship with the union employees in Bluffton went from adversarial to cooperative, proving that the right approach can pay off handsomely. On the other hand, the whole project collapsed because we failed to engage all of the stakeholders at the outset. We miscalculated the relationship the vice president of HR had with his counterpart in Italy. We thought his relationship was strong and the lines of communication were open. We found out later that Clark Campbell had not told the Italian HR office what we were doing in Bluffton.

We got carried away with the whole idea of a new approach to working with a union-represented workforce, and we totally overlooked how well, or poorly, the US management was working with the Italian parent company. We later found out that at the time we began discussing the situation with Clark Campbell, John Cooper, the president of North American operations, was on the short list for dismissal because of poor performance and failure to meet expected revenue and performance objectives.

Should we have been alert to these conditions? Absolutely! We were so excited about the opportunity to make a difference that we failed to follow our own rule— always involve *all* stakeholders.

Overall, we gave ourselves a B grade for this project. We indeed followed the approach diagrammed earlier, and for the most part it worked because we followed these basic principles of change:

- Follow the discipline of diagnosis before prescribing solutions.
- Engage all the stakeholders (we overlooked the foreign ownership of the company).
- Use data (evidence) to show the value of the change (improvement).

Our failure was in not ensuring that the foreign ownership was fully engaged and supportive, and it carried a very high price:

- Millions of dollars went down the drain.
- The plant was closed.
- Many employees lost their jobs.
- The community lost an important employer.

This successful change that failed left an indelible impression on both Scott and me. We made up our minds that this would never happen again. However, in our next project together, we discovered that one person can destroy an organization.

Story 9—One Person Can Destroy an Organization

by Scott Janoch

Under our guidance, the leaders of the Good Buy Groceries Company, the organization featured in this story, followed a diagnostic process in redesigning their company. They conducted a scan of their organization's data as a basis for understanding their readiness for change. This was followed by a four-phase approach that capitalized on the skills and ideas of the company's leadership staff (engagement). A design team was formed and developed a reorganization plan that they believed in and supported. The plan was presented to the CEO and his staff along with a new vice president for retail business. That's the point at which the whole endeavor went off the rails. The new VP, criticizing the efforts of the design team, singlehandedly shot down the entire project. Despite following a diagnostic approach, before our very eyes Glenn and I watched another successful change project go down the tubes.

Almost fifty years ago, a group of nine small, individually owned grocery stores was locked in a life-and-death struggle with the major grocery chains of the day. Their biggest problem was an inability to compete at the wholesale level. While the major chains could demand quantity discounts from wholesalers for everything from meat to laundry soap, the individually owned stores just weren't large enough to capture the lowest prices for the foods they sold to their customers. If things had continued in this fashion, these nine entrepreneurs would have had to watch their businesses wither and die.

Then one of them got the idea of forming a cooperative to pool their purchasing strength to lower the costs of their products. They became the Upper Midwest Grocery Cooperative and were able to successfully compete in a world of ever-expanding grocery giants. Before long, they were purchasing their goods at competitive prices and winning their customers back from the big-box grocery stores in town.

For more than twenty years, they prospered. Some

expanded to two or three stores, spreading to nearby towns. New independent stores joined the co-op, and as the number expanded, they all experienced increased sales and higher profits.

In the late 1970s, the co-op members decided to take the next step and become their own grocery distributor, supplying themselves as well as other stores in the upper Midwest. Gradually, the new business they began, Good Buy Groceries, grew in size until its profitability overshadowed that of the retail grocery stores owned by the individual members.

Things could have gone on this way, with everyone being better off, if one of the members hadn't decided that it was time for him to retire. He discussed retirement with his family and found that none of his children, in-laws, or grandchildren had any interest in taking over his store and remaining in the grocery business. He brought his problem to the next cooperative members' meeting and discovered that he wasn't the only one facing this dilemma. Many of the members were approaching retirement, and few had found family members who wanted to carry on the business.

The management of Good Buy Groceries realized that they too had a problem. If the co-op members were forced to close their stores when they reached retirement age, or sell them off to grocery chains that used other wholesalers, Good Buy Groceries would soon find that its customer base had melted away. Management's solution was to purchase the members' stores as they became available, and the four-billion-dollar wholesale food distributor entered the retail grocery field for the first time.

However, this meant that the organization faced

transforming itself from a wholesale food distributor into a fast-track, highly competitive, retail-oriented company. Even though they had some small-town retail store experience, they were no match for the "big boys" in retail grocery. To accomplish this feat, they needed help and guidance in systematically changing the organization. They had recently hired a vice president of human resources. I had worked for him for a time before becoming a consultant, and he recommended that the executives of Good Buy Groceries meet with Glenn and me to discuss their problem. An initial visit was scheduled, and we looked forward to the opportunity of working with a new industry.

Our first meeting took place at the company's headquarters and main distribution center. We met with the president/CEO and several of the executives and began gathering data to be used in making a preliminary assessment of the business and its operating conditions. Once completed, a number of interesting facts emerged:

- The company had already begun the acquisition of some of its smaller customers.
- The entire organization was anticipating a major reorganization of the company.
- There were a number of talented midlevel managers, and the executive team wanted to retain and develop them.
- Good Buy Groceries had previously used a different consulting firm to design and install a Total Quality Program (TQP) throughout the organization. The effort failed and left the company wary of consultants.

- There appeared to be openness at the managerial level to the introduction of innovative organizational ideas.
- The president/CEO was solidly behind the reorganization of the company, and he had obtained the backing of the board of directors for the process.

The conditions seemed ideal for our consulting firm, so Glenn and I next presented a proposal outlining a four-phase approach to the reorganization:

- Phase one was to be a self-study/assessment including a review of the company's
  - o internal capabilities;
  - o external environmental factors; and a
  - o competency evaluation and benchmarking.
- Phase two consisted of forming a design team made up of mid- and upper-level managers and staff members to redesign and recast the organization's structure, processes, and systems.
- Phase three was the installation of the design plan once the executive team and the board of directors had given their approval.
- Phase four would be the establishment of a monitoring and evaluation team to follow developments and recommend changes as the new organization evolved.

We proposed a cost for the accomplishment of the first two phases and estimated that it would take one to two years to complete them. The president/CEO, the executive team, and the board of directors reviewed the proposal and, with some minor adjustments, approved the proposal and gave us the go ahead.

With our assistance, the company assembled teams of mid- and upper-level managers and staff employees from throughout the organization to begin working on phase one. Forty team members, representing each of the four major distribution centers, were selected from the 1,500 members of the organization. They were divided into three working teams, and each team, facilitated by a consultant, was assigned to conduct a key portion of the analysis—a detailed internal assessment, an external environmental assessment, and a resource competency evaluation coupled with competition benchmarking.

Each week the three assessment teams met individually in a nearby Catholic retirement center to work on their portion of the project, and they sent representatives to a monthly meeting, held in the company's boardroom, to report their results and seek input from the other teams. A company newsletter was established, and the outcomes of the three assessment teams were summarized and reported monthly to all employees. The organization responded with enthusiasm and excitement. Some of the responses included, "The sleeping giant is finally waking up," and "This is going to work," and "It's about time they recognized the talent in the organization."

At the conclusion of their work, the three teams presented the results of their studies to the president/ CEO, the executive team, and the members of the board of directors in a one-day meeting. The key action items of their report included the need for

- a major reorganization;

- redeployment of staff;
- the acquisition of a top-level executive to manage the retail business;
- understanding the entry of significant competitors into markets where the company was purchasing smaller retail stores; and
- recognition of the fact that the company was significantly behind the competition in the application of technology and in management's understanding of new business ideas and concepts.

Following the feedback meeting, which was a resounding success, the president/CEO established a team for the purpose of designing a new organization, including the development of a new vision and mission statement and the changes required to achieve them. Under our guidance, this design team met almost full-time over a two-month period and produced a report that recommended the following Future Strategy Change Model:

Future Strategy Change Model

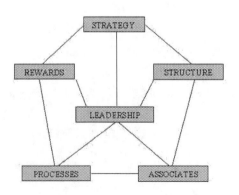

Each part of the model was discussed in great detail, including the specific changes recommended as well as the appropriate timing. While this team was meeting, the president/CEO recruited and hired a vice president for retail business. The new VP brought a number of years of direct sales experience in the grocery industry, and he had most recently served as the director of sales for a major northeastern grocery chain. At the conclusion of the team's work, the members and the consultants met with the president/CEO and the executive team, including the new vice president, to report the conclusions and explain what they were recommending the next steps should be. As the team completed its report, the new vice president for retail business took the floor.

He announced that he was currently negotiating for the acquisition of a large, privately held retail chain in a city in northwestern Ohio. He told those present that he had decided the design team would be disbanded and would cease all work on its reports, and he directed the members to return to their "real" jobs. "Based on my experience," he said, "if there is any reorganizing to be done, I will decide what to reorganize and when it will happen. I don't need any help in designing my organization. I am quite capable of captaining this ship on my own." The design team, the other company executives, and Glenn and I sat there in stunned silence—the president/CEO had no comment.

No reorganization took place, and the recommendations of the teams were ignored. The acquisition was completed as the VP had predicted, and Good Buy Groceries went public after merging the Ohio-based company into their existing structure.

The merged operations included approximately fifty-five

supermarkets and twenty-five deep-discount drugstores. After the merger, the stores continued to operate under their own banners, but heavy competition in areas where the supermarkets and pharmacies operated meant lower margins. These new stores proved to be a drain on the company's resources. Within two years, the company closed or sold sixteen of the supermarkets and half of the discount drugstores. One year later, with an unmanageable debt load, Good Buy Groceries announced that it was selling or closing all of the remaining supermarkets and drugstores and was planning to restructure the company. Shortly thereafter, the president/CEO and the vice president for retail business announced their resignations.

The Rest of the Story

The introduction of the new vice president for retail business into the organizational redesign process dealt a crippling blow to the organization. It was so devastating that the members of the company's design team threw up their hands and withdrew support that the president and VP for retail business critically needed to be successful. There was no way the VP for retail business could succeed without organizational support, especially at a time when the company needed all the help it could get to accomplish the successful acquisition of a large retail chain.

The earliest signs of failure were the timing of the acquisition and the board of directors' impatience with the reorganization process. The board had pressured the president/CEO to hire a retail "expert," and one of the design team's recommendations had been to do just that. However, the board wanted him to be hired quickly while they were considering an acquisition. The result was that the new VP for retail business had no knowledge of the strategic planning that was already underway and no interest in learning about it. His instructions from the board were simple: "Make the acquisition work no matter what." Those were his marching orders, and that's exactly what he intended to do, regardless of its effect on the overall organization. However, he overlooked one key point— the people who work for an organization are the ones who have to "make it work." He got no internal support; the staff withdrew and dug in their heels. A number of key managers resigned or got replaced. The effort was doomed.

The president/CEO felt he was powerless in all of this, because the board of directors was pushing the acquisition without organizational support. They didn't seem to care that a strategic planning process was underway that was widely supported in the organization.

Ironically, the vice president of human resources who introduced us to Good Buy Groceries was the same person who had been involved in the "Blah, Blah, Blah— You're Fired" project. In retrospect, we wondered why he hadn't been aware of the goings-on of the board of directors and the top rungs of the company. He should have been in the know, participating in the top-level decisions of the organization, specifically the recruitment of a vice president for retail business and the acquisition of a new business venture. Had he been aware of the changes taking place, we might have been able to adapt to the situation and educate and engage the new vice president in the process already underway.

Grasping the Situation after the Fact

So what did we learn from this experience?

- Working for a person/contact who is not included in the top-level thinking and actions is problematic.
- Given a chance to complete the project, the diagnostic process works. We gave ourselves an A for design and an F for successful completion.
- Judging from the interest and support of the management, staff, and employees, clearly engaging those involved in the process is essential if the change is to work.

It seemed that grasping the situation didn't necessarily ensure success. However, in the next story, we thought we were finally on track. As it turned out, we continued to misjudge the key players, the decision leaders, and their role in success or failure. In this situation, the human resources VP was a strong person who pushed other leaders in the organization to change their ways. However, he failed to recognize that in his organization he was viewed as a people helper, not a strategic thinker, and we missed it too. We continued to view key leaders through the eyes and minds of our clients (in most cases the human resources VP) rather than making our own assessments. That is, until we lived through "A Know-It-All Leader Crashes and Burns."

Story 10—A Know-It-All Leader Crashes and Burns

This is the story of a vice president of distribution who paid dearly for his failure to use his good-scientist skills and change his know-it-all attitude. It is told from his first-hand perspective.

My name is A. Frank Wit, and this is my story about how, as the result of a life-changing career crisis, I learned too late the correct way to change an organization. I graduated from high school about the time of Desert Storm, and with all of the patriotic intensity of an eighteen-year-old, I joined the Marine Corps for a three-year hitch. During a tour overseas, I rose to the rank of sergeant.

After my discharge, I attended college and graduated with a degree in industrial engineering. I felt that my training in IE would position me to work in a manufacturing firm where I could put my skills to good use organizing and designing work systems that would produce high performance. I found employment as a systems engineer for a company that produced molded plastic parts. Within ten years, I was a supervisor on my way up the management ladder.

By this time, I had formed a set of ideas about managing that I firmly believed would work to improve efficiency and performance results in any organization. For example, I believed that:

- A disciplined and direct personal style was the best way to manage and control output.
- System efficiency was the most effective way to keep costs down.

- The workforce had to be well trained in operations, and specifically in their immediate jobs.
- Strong and tight supervision is required to immediately correct workforce and operational problems.
- The customer's needs are always first, especially when it comes to producing high-quality products, and they must always be delivered on time.
- Reward/punishment is the best way to motivate people.
- Keeping up to date requires continuous bench-marking and utilizing the latest tools and practices, such as zero defects, lean manufacturing, supply chain concepts, and the like.

These principles worked well for me as I advanced in the organization, and I was ultimately promoted to vice president of distribution. In this position, I was responsible for four large product-warehousing operations. Everything seemed to go well for the first two or three years. We had an acceptable number of returns and complaints from customers (missed delivery dates, incorrect product mix, items missing from orders, etc.). Turnover was a little higher than I would have liked, but overall I thought everything was under control.

Then one day I received a call from the vice president of human resources. She advised me that we had a union-organizing attempt underway in our largest distribution center, located In South Carolina. She said we needed to get on this problem *right now* in order to "head off the union." She also suggested I hire two consultants to guide me through the process. With their advice and assistance,

I attacked the situation head-on and put a number of measures in place:

- We initiated a union-avoidance program involving the entire workforce of 110 associates.
- We began supervisory training in how to communicate with and manage the workforce.
- We introduced a series of work-group roundtable meetings with associates to solicit their concerns, complaints, and ideas.
- We installed a gainsharing program designed to reward associate contributions.
- We began training in the use of lean tools and practices for the workforce.
- We increased inventories to ensure that we could meet our customers' needs.

I was certain that another part of the problem was my distribution center (DC) manager. He was weak and needed to be more forceful in his relationships with the workforce. However, he insisted that he was on top of it and that he knew his associates. I disagreed and told him that he had thirty days to get it right or find another employer.

Things went from bad to worse. I received reports that the union-organizing drive was moving forward and picking up steam, customer complaints were up, and we were not meeting budget. The gainsharing plan that we had designed to get the workforce to line up with management looked like it was going to give away the shop. Worst of all, from my point of view, our biggest customer called the president, raising hell about quality, missed delivery times, product errors, and so on.

With all of these problems threatening, I decided that it was time for me to move into the distribution center and take personal charge of the situation. As soon as I arrived, I took the following actions:

- I dismissed the consultants and changed the gainsharing formula to reduce the economic impact on the distribution center.
- I reorganized the associates' shift patterns.
- I initiated the associate position of "checker" to audit all shipments to customers.
- I terminated several of the supervisors who seemed to be sympathetic to the union.
- I froze all salary increases.
- I made it known that if productivity didn't increase and costs decrease, heads would roll.

Things didn't improve. Performance continued to deteriorate. We began to get threats from the customers that they would take their business elsewhere if things didn't get better, and fast. The union showed no signs of backing off their organizing attempt. Finally, I got a call from the company president saying that he was coming to the distribution center to look into the mess himself. He arrived with the vice president of human resources, and they spent one full day on the floor of the operation. At the end of the day, I was given my walking papers!

Look Out Below

What a blow to my ego. I just couldn't believe that all the experience I had gained, and all that I had learned in my career, had failed me. I was out of work for six months, during which time I met with a career counselor who suggested, "Maybe you should be looking at yourself as the source of the problem. Don't you realize that as an engineer, you have scientific skills and should be using them in handling situations like this? All you had to do was follow the lead and the advice of the consultants." His words shocked me; I had never thought about myself in this way.

The Rest of the Story

The day after Frank was separated from the company, we received a call from the VP of human resources. She had just completed a walk-through of the facility, and after talking to more than twenty associates, she concluded that the original plan had been working. The associates she had spoken with represented a good cross section of the workforce, and they were especially thrilled by the gainsharing plan. She asked if we could help her put the programs and practices we had initially set up, and that Frank had recently discarded, back in effect.

Because Frank's new changes had not really become effective yet, it was relatively easy to put everything back in place. Once Frank was out of the picture, the DC manager came out of hiding and took a strong leadership role in getting things back on track. Within six months, performance indicators were beginning to improve, customer complaints were down, and most importantly, the union was rejected by a large majority of the DC's associates.

The key to this success was the gainsharing plan. It engaged the associates and gained their support, which resulted in associate-sponsored improvements and significant financial gain for all the associates, the DC, and the company.

Grasping the Situation after the Fact

As the consultant in this story, I kept asking myself, "How many times do I have to make the same mistakes?" So I took a look at why I repeated the mistake of misjudging the leader's intent, and I got a rude awakening. I suspected most leaders had other plans but disregarded my suspicions because I thought I could outsmart the client leader. Lesson learned: deal with leader intent up front, before starting any project. The leader (client) must always be on board for a change project to succeed. This seemed to me like a never-ending learning experience. Among the other takeaways, I learned/relearned:

- Always test the client to determine his/her level of commitment to the change.
- Hold the client's hand when the going gets rough, as it almost always will at first.
- The diagnostic process works because it grasps the true situation and engages the stakeholders in making the change work.

It took me one more project to finally realize that "When the leader isn't on board, forget it." There is no excuse for another failure because of uncommitted leadership.

Glenn H. Varney, PhD

Story 11—When the Leader
Isn't on Board, Forget It

Here is a story about a change project where everything
seemed to be working as planned. The plant processes
were studied, the diagnostic approach was followed, and
the intervention was thoroughly planned. The employees
were engaged in the planning, and they tested the
effectiveness of the proposed changes. However, once
the change was designed and the entire plant was excited
and ready to go, the plant manager shot the plan down
and installed his own changes, with poor results. Here
is the story from the company's vice president of human
resources.

The plant manager of one of our small, hundred-
plus employee manufacturing plants needed help. At my
insistence, he contacted Glenn and Scott and explained
that he was trying to find ways to build on a Total Quality
Program (TQP) that was based on a self-managing team
(SMT) concept that was already in place at his factory.
A date and time was established, and the two of them
met with the plant manager and me at our corporate
headquarters.

I explained that the plant had implemented a total quality
program several years ago, and employee work teams
were presently functioning without direct supervisors. "We
need to teach our people how to work in teams more
effectively in order to generate ways to improve overall
plant performances," I said. "You have a reputation for

delivering performance improvement through teaming initiatives, and that's just the kind of training we need."

Glenn and Scott explained that to be sure what was being taught would actually improve plant performances, they would need to collect information about current production processes, plant policies, employee attitudes, and other elements that affected performance at this particular operation. Once that information had been gathered, a strategy could be developed for improvement.

After a brief discussion, the plant manager and I agreed and asked for a proposal and a cost estimate. Several days later, the consultants submitted their assessment proposal. The company accepted, and the assessment phase of the process began.

The consultants constructed an outside assessment team using local student interns from the graduate program of a nearby university. They collected information about the organizational structure, performance measures, demographics, employee attitudes, plant policies and procedures, and so on. After consolidating and analyzing the data, the following conclusions were reached:

- The plant had self-managing teams in name only. Employees did not feel that they were free to make management decisions.
- The plant operated on a twenty-four-hour-per-day, seven-day-per-week basis.
- There were two ineffective supervisors directing operations in the production department.
- Most of the human resources policies and the organizational leadership style did not

support self-managing teams or a performance-improvement process.
- The total quality program seemed to be somewhat effective in generating process improvements that contributed to increases in plant performance.

This information was summarized in a report and submitted to the plant manager, with a copy to me, accompanied by a new proposal and cost estimate. This proposal recommended the following steps:

- Go back to the drawing board and redesign the self-managing team concept.
- Involve as many employees in the redesign process as possible to build support and commitment.
- Delay any training until the new organizational plan has been designed and implemented.

I accepted the proposal, and, somewhat reluctantly, the plant manager agreed. A design team was formed at the plant and, with a consultant facilitating, we began meeting on a regular basis to accomplish the following objectives:

- Learn how to organize self-managing productivity teams.
- Benchmark other organizations using self-managing teams.
- Conduct an internal assessment to determine the organization's state of readiness for self-managing teams.
- Design an implementation plan based on the assessment conducted by the design team.

Upon completion of these tasks, the design team recommended a major overhaul of the organization, including the following:

- Establishing four twelve-hour shift teams;
- Giving the shift teams responsibility for managing themselves, including scheduling, process improvements, safety, overtime distribution, vacation scheduling, and the like;
- Having each team select its own team coordinator;
- Establishing a leadership team composed of management, staff, and the team coordinators, with responsibility for overseeing and coordinating the operation of the plant; and
- Establishing a gain-sharing plan.

This proposal was very different from what the plant manager had been expecting. However, the plant and staff employees were strongly supportive of the proposal, and, with my approval, the plant manager reluctantly gave the go-ahead to implement the recommendations.

One year later, it was time to evaluate the plan and its outcomes. All employees completed an audit survey, and the results indicated that the plan was 75 percent operational. The gainsharing plan was making a regular quarterly payout, and plant performances showed steady improvement.

Nine months after that, the gainsharing plan was reviewed. The review revealed flaws in the original design, including a failure to link/integrate the Total Quality Plan with team performance improvements. Employees reported that they found it difficult to see how their suggestions under the TQP would translate into gainsharing payout dollars. Modifications were made to the gainsharing plan, and it seemed to improve the linkage between gainsharing and the TQP.

Throughout the process, the plant manager resisted employees' suggestions and changes, and he attempted to block employee improvement ideas. For example, several of the employee operators proposed changes to the reporting systems, and he flatly refused to consider them, with no explanation given. One day, about eighteen months after the initial implementation, corporate headquarters installed a new production metrics plan that rendered the gainsharing plan's measures invalid. By focusing corporate attention on different plant performance measures to determine how the various plants compared with each other, the metrics that had been so carefully developed by the employees became irrelevant in the scheme of things. Despite almost two years of building employee-generated performance improvements, the plant manager scrapped the self-managing team concept and returned to the old top-down, supervisor-driven management structure. One year later, we sold the plant.

The Rest of the Story

As consultants, we went away licking our wounds. In our eagerness to get the contract, we overlooked, or perhaps ignored, telltale signs of a leader who had decided before we even started that he would shut the process down at the first opportunity.

The project followed sound change management principles by collecting data about the organization before designing the actual change process. We involved the stakeholders and monitored the process, making necessary adjustments as we went along. However, we consistently failed to identify the subtle hand of the plant manager as he undermined the process day by day. Whenever anyone—employees, supervisors, or consultants—wanted to discuss changes or suggestions, the plant manager would always claim that he was doing what was best for the plant and its customers. What he really meant was that he was doing what his manufacturing VP in headquarters was telling him to do. We saw this as indifference on his part and tried to get the plant manager to take a more proactive and supportive role, but in this we were unsuccessful.

For the associates, it was a cruel and unfair engagement, and it is easy to blame the plant manager, the human resources VP, and the consultants. We were wrong to allow the process to move forward in light of the plant manager's resistance.

Grasping the Situation after the Fact

I also failed to understand the complicated relationship the plant manager had with the human resources VP and the manufacturing VP. Hindsight suggests that it is wise to know your clients before you begin a change project. Therefore:

- Don't ever begin if you doubt that you can succeed;

- Test the leader's commitment from start to finish, and stop when that commitment ceases; and
- The basic principle of change management—and especially the diagnostic process—works, but only if leadership agrees.

In the next story, we found that a diagnostic process worked but wasn't implemented and was then forgotten. It's a good example of learning and then failing to apply what has been learned.

Story 12—The Diagnostic Process Worked but Was Then Forgotten

Blending a well-established culture with a new team-focused management style can work, provided that you apply the diagnostic process correctly and consistently. That means grasping the *current* situation, designing an intervention, and then applying it properly.

In this story, a very bright accountant-turned-CEO commissioned a method for selecting associates who would fit into a newly blended culture. It would have worked well if it had been used when hiring associates for a new facility. However, failure to implement the selection method eventually resulted in the employees being organized by a union and in the ultimate downsizing of the facility.

We consulted with the CEO in this situation, and here is the true story of what happened.

Walt Meyer received his bachelor of science degree in accounting from a major Midwestern university, and he was promptly hired as a staff accountant at a top accounting firm. Although he initially enjoyed the work, after several years he became dissatisfied with the lack of career advancement. He wanted to make the transition from general accounting into organizational leadership. Walt decided that he needed additional educational credentials to fulfill his goal, so he enrolled in the executive MBA program at a nearby college. Two years later, his freshly minted MBA degree in hand, he began looking for a leadership position with a firm specializing in finance and accounting.

It took Walt three months to be hired as the assistant to the chief financial officer (CFO) of We Care, Inc., an assisted-living organization owned by a large Protestant church. His boss, the CFO, was impressed with Walt's drive and abilities, and he recommended Walt as his replacement when he retired eighteen months later. *Wow!* Walt thought. *I have finally arrived.*

Now, Walt was no ordinary CFO. Although he held a responsible senior management position, his ambitions were greater than simply running the money side of the business. He had his eye on general management, and in another two years he had advanced to executive vice president, administrative services. In his new position, he was responsible for the organization's finance, accounting, information technology, and human resources. This is where the story begins to get interesting.

We Care, Inc. was planning to introduce a new business model for assisted-living facilities. They intended to focus on their clients in a personal, individual manner. Instead of facilities based on a large, multibed hospital model, their new facilities would consist of clusters of large, freestanding homes, five per location, which would house individuals needing periodic care. As part of his executive vice president responsibilities, Walt was assigned the task of developing, building, and staffing a number of these cluster home facilities.

We Care, Inc. was already operating several facilities based on the older multibed hospital model, and they had established a caring and people-oriented culture that serviced these facilities very well. Walt was responsible for introducing a team-focused management approach into the new cluster home concept while staffing each five-house unit with ten dedicated associates per house—a total of fifty new associates per location. Recognizing how important it was for this new approach to be successful, Walt contacted us for assistance and advice.

To ensure that this expansion was completed following a diagnostic process, we recommended that Walt hire a group of graduate advanced psychology students associated with the Industrial and Organizational Psychology Department at the local university. They were asked to study We Care, Inc.'s current well-established culture and to recommend ways to blend the new team-focused management with the existing organization. Walt also commissioned them to design a survey that could be used in selecting people to be hired into the new cluster home units. The survey was to be designed following standard psychometric practices so as to comply with Equal Employment Opportunity Commission (EEOC) requirements and to ensure that each new hire would be a good cultural fit for the existing We Care, Inc. organization.

After the survey had been tested and validated as a reliable method for identifying individuals applying for positions in the new concept facilities, we recommended using it consistently for filling all positions—associates, staff, and management. When used in recruiting, it would greatly improve the chances that a new hire would fit into the already well-established culture of the organization.

In the middle of all of this activity, Walt had another major career opportunity. The president and CEO of We Care, Inc. announced that he would be retiring at the beginning of the new year, and the board of directors was considering Walt as his replacement. Walt's record of developing and initiating the new cluster home concept argued positively for his promotion. The board members agreed that he had demonstrated strong leadership skills, and within six months, Walt was appointed president and CEO of We Care, Inc.

Walt was well organized, and he began establishing effective controls on his organization's performance. The first cluster home location, Green Tree Acres, was completed, staffed, and opened to the public on time and under budget, and Walt moved his attention to breaking ground at four other sites. But a few months later, a challenge arose when the state's accrediting agency inspected the Green Tree Acres facility. They cited the following concerns:

- New associates were ineffectively trained.
- There were contradictory and confusing decision-making procedures involving patient care in the "home health" environment.
- Because the cluster homes contained homelike appearances, finishes, and monitoring systems, although they met I-9 occupancy standards, the

accrediting agency raised questions about the quality of service in this new environment.

There were other concerns expressed regarding the operation of Green Tree Acres, but they were not considered by the accrediting agency to be significant. Walt discovered that the managers charged with recruiting staff for the new cluster home facilities were selecting and training new associates using the traditional methods of interviews, background screens, and peer-to-peer shadowing. The survey, designed to ensure that new employees were a good culture fit, was not being used at all. Because the organization was church-based, the new hires needed to be caring, thoughtful, socially oriented, and collaborative. Instead they were hiring associates based only on their technical skills, without any consideration being given to their social skills.

Having the state agency question some of the operating practices of the facility was not the only challenge at Green Tree Acres. The team-focused management style was new to the organization. Walt and the other members of his executive team had failed to consider just how different this new style would be. Integrating the new management style into the organization's existing culture was a complicated process, and the turnover at Green Tree Acres was much higher than they had expected. The executive team had anticipated an even lower turnover rate in the new facility than they had been experiencing in their more traditional settings. When the increased turnover and its attendant costs became known to the board of directors, they were not pleased.

Not only was Green Tree Acres experiencing higher

turnover of nurses and nurses' aides, even the director of nursing, who had been hired to supervise the facility, tendered her resignation. This was very troubling to Walt and the executive team. They had expected their new team-focused management approach to be popular with the staff at all levels, and this was not proving to be the case.

Walt set out to discover the cause of the problem. After reviewing the facility's policies and procedures, he concluded that the training being given to the new associates was ineffective, entry-level pay was inadequate, and the facility leadership was not supporting a team-centered environment. He completely overlooked the fact that the survey, which had been developed to ensure recruitment of candidates who would fit the culture of We Care, Inc., was not being utilized.

Walt, struggling to overcome these problems and regain the board's confidence in his ability to lead We Care, Inc., replaced the organization's director of human resources not once but twice! He expanded his executive team by hiring a vice president of operations, John Smith, and made him directly responsible for the new cluster home facilities. Neither Walt nor any of the other members of the executive team considered the issue of cultural fit as a possible culprit for the problems being experienced.

The issue of social skills never seemed to enter the minds of the newer additions to the management staff. As a result, new associates were hired without any consideration of how well these new people would fit into the organization. Walt and his executive team were blindsided by the next development—an international union began an organizing drive among the nurses and nurses' aides at Green Tree Acres.

The leadership team for the new cluster home facilities consisted of Sally Oster, the executive director; Josh Born, the teaming coach; and Millicent Sampson, the new director of nursing. Because of timing and the need to overcome the high turnover, this team had hired new associates using the "we need a warm body now" approach. The result of this ill-considered selection process was the hiring of personnel who did not understand or appreciate the organization's culture, and these new associates resisted many of the patient initiatives that management was trying to install. In addition, inadequate screening had resulted in the hiring of nursing staff members with experience in well-established union environments. These employees planned to introduce unionization into the new cluster home facility. The facility leadership team found themselves battling a union-organizing drive, and they were ill prepared to win the hearts and minds of the new associates.

We Care, Inc.'s executive team had no experience with union-organizing efforts either, and they turned to their new vice president of human resources for assistance. Unfortunately, Louis Good, whom Walt had recently hired for this position, had minimal experience with unions. There was no doubt that the union had found a fertile field to plow.

As part of his duties as vice president of operations, John Smith was expected to visit each of the cluster home facilities at least weekly to keep in touch with developments and look for solutions to problems. Instead he began to lengthen the time between these visits until they became monthly tours rather than weekly problem-solving visits. He almost seemed disinterested. His behavior served to isolate and alienate the leadership team at Green Tree Acres, and it resulted in increasing friction between the associates and leadership. The associates were seeking to discuss their concerns with leadership, but leadership was unresponsive.

Driven to seek outside help with the union-organizing drive, Walt chose to engage a well-known law firm for assistance and advice. The attorneys implemented all of the union-avoidance techniques in their bag of tricks while the facility's leadership team stood by, watching the show. When the lawyers' tactics, unsupported by the local leadership team, failed, the union succeeded in winning the representation election by a significant percentage. We Care, Inc. blamed the union, but the truth is that the fate of Green Tree Acres had been determined long before the union representation vote was taken. The facility's selection practices had resulted in a significant group of associates who simply did not fit the We Care, Inc. culture, and the organization was paying the steep price.

The union, capitalizing on its victory at Green Tree Acres, began efforts to organize the remaining cluster home sites and then planned to attack the more traditional facilities operated by We Care, Inc. Walt dismissed the local attorneys and hired a high-powered consultant with a reputation as a union buster. Together they began a struggle to keep the union out of the remaining locations.

This whole episode cost We Care, Inc. hundreds of thousands of dollars, control of the workforce at Green Tree Acres, and the anguish of fighting a union corporate campaign. All of this might have been avoided if Walt and his executive team had properly valued the importance of culture and fit in the screening and recruiting of new associates at all levels of the organization.

The Rest of the Story

As Walt put it, "I should have seen this coming. I did not pay attention to the most important part of my new responsibilities, making sure I got the right people in the right jobs to fit the culture that had worked so well in the past." Instead, it was a painful process retrofitting his organization. It required a lot of people being released and new people being recruited.

Because Walt recognized the cultural strengths in his organization, and he hired a union-buster consultant to lead the activity, he was successful in winning elections in the other facilities. In order to minimize the effect of unionization at the Green Tree Acres facility, where the union had won its election, Walt began to reduce the staff and the number of patients while negotiations for the first union agreement were ongoing. The union interpreted this as a prelude to the closing of the facility. When the union saw the writing on the wall, it abandoned the new unit and withdrew. The union representative stated, "It just isn't worth the investment."

Grasping the Situation after the Fact

I helped the client diagnose the problem and design the tools to assure a productive and caring culture. I followed these steps:

- Recognizing the problem (symptoms).

- Collecting data and clearly defining the present, effective culture.
- Testing the measurement instruments (validate, validate, validate).
- Encouraging use of the new selection survey and process.

However, the ball was dropped because of organizational changes (Walt becoming CEO and the replacement of several vice presidents of human resources). Policies, practices, and installation training were never completed.

It was our suspicion that Walt used the cluster housing project to advance his own career. He was vying for the top job and not paying attention to the cultural mixing process (intervention) as new associates were hired.

From this last series of stories, I learned that the diagnostic approach works. However, if the top leader isn't using good scientist skills in his or her reasoning and decision making, it can lead to failure.

In the next section of this book, what I have learned from these mostly failed stories/projects is summarized and organized to put it all into understandable context. My hope is that demonstrating how I made mistakes can teach you how to avoid them.

Success with Leading Change Phase V

Learning from James M. McFillen and
Using Science to Grasp the Situation

At this point in my career, I was beginning to feel more confident about my ability to initiate organizational change that worked. Part of what made me feel this confidence was the fact that I had just completed a project I had been working on that had positive effects on the performance of the client organization. Teaming up with a savvy leader and an internal change agent, we successfully implemented a major organizational change applying a series of steps that followed the scientific process.

This is where Jim McFillen entered the stage. I had related this success story to Jim, and he decided to use it in a graduate course he was scheduled to teach. His idea was to use the story as the primary learning method to teach graduate students the steps in the change process. He invited me to co-teach the course, which provided me with an opportunity to validate the change steps I had followed in the actual situation.

This true story was used successfully over a span of two to three years with many discussions and reworks over tea/coffee, during which we continued to refine the change model.

In this phase of the book, I'll examine the science-based change process in more detail and reflect on the mind-set that consultants and leaders should have to make the process work.

As I examined my record of working with leaders, I estimated that about 60 to 70 percent of my projects had encountered unforeseen difficulties, generally due to faulty decisions made by the organization's leaders. I also recognized that my success increased as I gained more experience. It took me years to learn how to improve my batting average through lots of mistakes and false starts. Hopefully, it won't take as long for you, although you will make mistakes as you progress.

To explain the improvement, I took a closer look at each of the projects. What I discovered was that over time, the way I approached change evolved. Initially I followed a four-step process:

Contracting	Assessment	Feedback/Testing	Intervention Design
1	2	3	4

I began to realize that sometimes the intervention I designed to solve a problem turned out to be a waste of time and resources and often generated resistance to future change projects. This prompted me to question why the intervention had failed. My investigation revealed that I had designed a solution that fit the problem as it was defined by the client leader with whom I was working. So I began to ask myself, "Where am I getting off track?" The answer glared out at me: the problem wasn't with the solution; it was in not defining the problem correctly. That's a serious mistake to make. It was at the point when I joined Jim in teaching that I realized I was close to doing it right. Working with Jim cleared up confusion for me and led to the following five-step process:

1		2		3		4		5
Recognizing the Problem	→	Collecting and Synthesizing Relevant Symptoms	→	Formulating a Preliminary Diagnosis	→	Testing the Preliminary Diagnosis	→	Intervention Design

This later became the model described in the article "Organizational Diagnosis—An Evidence-Based Approach." I realized that how you think about your ability to make positive change depends a lot on the mind-set you work with every day.

The following story illustrates how a leader came to realize that he already had the science-based model in his mind but that he was only using it on technical matters of change.

Story 13—The Science Model in Action—A Learning Example

David Brown, a good friend of mine who was a highly successful executive in a major US corporation, told me a story about a leader who discovered how to use his scientific skills in solving organizational problems. I thought you would find this story eye opening. It's told by Wendell Deworth, the president of a midsized (two thousand employees) auto parts manufacturer.

———————————

This learning event occurred when Dave and I were on a walk-through of our main plant. I was particularly interested in having him see a new piece of production equipment that we had just purchased and installed. This machine was designed to improve our output by as much as 20 percent, and we estimated a full return on our investment in about three months. You can imagine how interested I was in its commissioning.

As I got to the production area, I noted that the machine was not operating, so I asked my plant engineer what was happening.

"I just can't seem to get it up to full capacity," he said.

I immediately stepped in to see if I could spot the difficulty and started looking for symptoms that would help me identify the problem. I tested several things and discovered that the control monitor was the culprit. Within twenty minutes, I had solved the problem, and the machine was running flat-out. I was pleased with myself, and it was kind of fun too.

Expecting Dave to approve of what I had done, I was surprised at the look of distress on his face. We headed back to the conference room, and I was very interested in what Dave would have to say. As we got our coffee and sat down across the table from each other, Dave said, "Why did you do that?"

"Why did I do what?" I asked. "Do you mean why did I solve that machine problem?"

"That's exactly what I mean," said Dave.

"When that machine is down, it is costing us money, and we had to get it up and running ASAP," I replied.

Dave raised his voice. "That's not what I mean! I'm asking you why *you* fixed the machine."

"Well," I said, "there is no one else who understands this problem like I do, so I jumped in."

By now Dave had grown impatient with me, and he said, "Why you? Don't you have qualified people trained to do that kind of work? Why should an executive like you, the company president, be messing around in a day-to-day operating problem? Aren't you supposed to be leading this organization into the future? Why are you wasting your valuable time doing someone else's work?"

I didn't know how to respond. Dave just kept asking me questions like, "Are you sure you're the only person in your entire organization who can fix this problem? Did you notice how your engineer stepped back and folded his arms? Did you see the look on his face, like he was saying to himself, 'Okay, if you're so good, you do it'? Not only that, but did you see the two other staff employees turn away and head back to their offices? Even the machine operator moved away, shaking his head as if to say, 'He's doing it again.'"

After about an hour of back-and-forth discussion with Dave, I finally realized that because I have the unique ability to spot the cause of an engineering problem, I always tend to jump in and fix the problem. Dave went on to explain that I learned this scientific-based approach as an engineer but that I don't use this insight when working with people in my organization. He recommended that I start using my scientific skills in the way I run my company.

It's simple; use your scientific skills to solve problems when you are making organizational change. Here's how William B. Wolf ("The Parable of Diagnostics," *Journal of Organizational Change Management* 7, no. 3 [1994]: 6–7) explains how to develop your scientific skills:

> My explanation is that through deep involvement and intensive experience one learns to react to minimum clues, to notice

what is incongruent, and to recognize what is experienced, felt, and thought—like a good scientist who gathers data, forms hypotheses, checks them for congruence with various aspects of the phenomenon, and recognizes interdependencies.

Developing Your Good Scientist

To understand what your "good scientist" is, I begin with a definition. A scientist is a person who has knowledge and skill/proficiency in a specific field (medicine, engineering, etc.) and who follows the scientific method in discovering new approaches and solutions to problems and making change. The scientific method follows "Principles and procedures for systematic pursuit of knowledge involving the recognition and formulation of a problem, the collection of data through observation, and experimentation, and the formulation and testing of hypotheses" (Merriam-Webster's Collegiate Dictionary, 11th ed.).

Organizational leaders and change agents use their good scientist skills by following and applying the scientific method to solve problems faster and more efficiently, resulting in a much higher success rate.

Physicians, engineers, and scientists use the five-step method shown on page 138 and begin with steps one and two—recognizing that there is a problem to be solved and gathering data about it. In the case of a physician, a patient complains of pain or a general feeling of ill health. For the engineer, step one begins when something is not working the way it was designed to work. For the scientist, whether it is a human disease or a problem in space travel, the first thing is recognizing that a problem exists. For each one, this recognition triggers the gathering of all relevant information associated with the problem. From data collection, they move to developing a cause-and-effect statement or a prediction (a hypothesis), and then they test the prediction to check its validity. If it is valid, the process continues with the doctor, engineer, or the scientist designing an intervention to alleviate the problem. Finally, they test the intervention to see if it has solved the problem.

Let's go back to Wendell Deworth to see how he applied his good scientist persona to his situation. As you will recall, Wendell was an engineer trained in system diagnostics. He also had a deep involvement and extensive experience, which over the years taught him to recognize problems with minimal data. In diagnosing the machine problem, he quickly ruled out a number of variables that might have been the culprit and narrowed the problem to two or three possible causes. He concluded that either the speed control on the machine was defective or the control monitor was malfunctioning. He checked the speed control and discovered that it was working properly, so that left the control monitor. He opened the control-monitor panel and removed a computer chip, replacing it with a new one. The machine then started to run flat-out.

When reviewing Wendell's process, one notices that he was able to quickly move through the steps of the scientific method. Confronted with a machine problem, he applied the five steps:

1. Recognizing the problem

2. Collecting and synthesizing relevant symptoms (data)
3. Formulating a preliminary diagnosis
4. Testing the preliminary diagnosis
5. Intervention design

By following these steps, he resolved the problem, and the equipment was back up and running.

You may be wondering why Wendell's plant engineer didn't follow the same process and solve the problem himself. The plant engineer was new on the job and was unfamiliar with the equipment. He was also hesitant to tackle the problem in front of his boss, as he had already tried and was having trouble identifying the cause. In addition, in Wendell's estimation, no one else could understand the problem the way he did.

What Wendell learned from his encounter with Dave was that the scientific method works for all types of problems in all fields, including managing and leading.

Applying the Scientific Method in Organizations

Using the scientific process to grasp the situation in your organization can help you to fail-proof yourself as you make change decisions. Here are the steps to follow when you practice using your good scientist skills:

- *Recognizing that a problem exists.* This is easy because there is usually a trigger symptom that calls the problem to your attention. A trigger symptom is an event, behavior, statement, or action that signals that you may have a problem. It's like an alarm going off. When a trigger symptom is identified, the impulse to take immediate action is powerful and almost always leads to misdiagnosis and implementation of the wrong intervention.

- *Collecting and synthesizing relevant symptoms (data).* There are two kinds of symptoms you should be looking for:
  - o *Predictive symptoms* are events, words, and/or actions that forecast future problems.
  - o *Causal symptoms* are policies, procedures, practices, and management actions (decisions, culture, leadership style, etc.) that alter human reactions and behavior, giving rise to the problem you are diagnosing. For example, a supervisor decides without prior warning that his/her staff will be required to work overtime tonight.
- *Formulating a preliminary diagnosis* by organizing the symptoms, studying and weighing their relative importance, and finally arranging them in a cause-and-effect framework. This formalizes what you think is happening and explains what you think is going on in the organization.
- When the preliminary diagnosis has been formulated, the next step is *testing the preliminary diagnosis* to assure the description of the problem is accurate. This most necessary step can be done in a variety of ways, including asking questions to validate the information, surveying/checking

records, and sometimes gaining direct access to the trigger event and tracking it back to square one.

- Once the diagnosis is confirmed, the final step is *designing an intervention, applying it, and then testing to see what effect the intervention had on the problem.* The testing portion of this step is critical to effective problem solving/change management.

Grasp the Situation—A Story in Point

This is a true story about a single mother who worked as a member of a small-appliance new-product design team. She brought to the team an expertise in competitor-based design technology. Her name was Marie, and she had worked for the company for eight years. She had a seven-year-old daughter who had started second grade a few weeks ago.

Marie had a reputation of going the extra mile, the kind of person who makes significant contributions to innovative breakthroughs in design. Team members gave her high marks for "always being there when we need her." She had a record of always being in the office fifteen to twenty minutes before the others and eating her packed lunch on the job.

Recently Marie had begun showing up to work exactly at 8:00 a.m. She would come racing into the design center, throwing her coat on the table as she entered the room to meet her team. Several team members teased her with remarks such as, "Now you are behaving just like the rest of us." One team member also noticed that she had stopped bringing her lunch and was eating from the vending machines instead. Her group leader wondered what had changed her routine, but he never bothered to ask.

This went on for several weeks. Then one morning Marie showed up fifteen minutes late! Her tardiness continued for the remainder of the week. As she was leaving the office one afternoon, Mike, her group leader, asked her, "When are you going to get back on track and start getting here on time? Your tardiness is causing all kinds of problems for the team."

Marie replied, "I know, and I will try to do better." With that, she left.

The next week the same tardiness pattern continued. On Thursday, not only tardy, but she left thirty minutes early. The following morning, Mike took her aside to coach her. This time he was more forceful. "Marie, it's time for you to make a decision. Either you're an equal partner on the team or you're not. Be here on time starting next week." She was shocked, and she was crying when she left.

The following week, despite the coaching, the same pattern continued; she was late every day. The rest of the team members were complaining, and Mike decided to speak to his boss, Wilbur. Wilbur expressed concern and told Mike to have Marie stop by his office so that he could discuss the situation with her. He planned to explain to her the consequences of her recent behavior.

Marie showed up at Wilbur's office a little late. She sat down, and Wilbur said to her, "Do you know, Marie, that your team wants me to let you go because they cannot count on you anymore? What do you think I should do, Marie?"

Marie slouched in her chair, began sobbing, and

exclaimed, "I don't know what to do. I just don't know what to do."

Here is how Wilbur applied his good scientist skills to solve the problem:

1. **Recognizing the Problem**	*The problem came to head when Mike decided to get Wilbur involved. This would be classified as the trigger symptom.*

2.
Collecting and Synthesizing Relevant Symptoms (Data)
	Predictive Symptoms:
	    Marie's change from being early to work to arriving on time
	    Marie's tardiness
	    Marie stopped bringing her lunch
	    Marie's leaving early on a Thursday
	    Marie's positive past work record
	
	Causal Symptoms:
	    Single mother
	    Second-grader starting school
	    Time of year

3. **Formulating a Preliminary Diagnosis**	*There has been a change in Marie's family situation causing her to be late to work.*

4. **Testing the Preliminary Diagnosis**	*Wilbur met with Marie and asked her what was causing her to be late to work. In this case, Marie explained that her daughter took the bus to school, and until a week ago she had been able to get to work on time after she helped her daughter get on the bus. A week ago, the school changed the pickup time because they had to add a second stop. That meant her daughter had to get on the bus fifteen minutes later. This caused Marie to be fifteen minutes late. Then on that Thursday, she had to attend a school conference that began immediately after school ended.*
5. **Intervention Design**	*Wilbur decided to meet with Mike to explain the situation and then talk with the rest of the team about the changes Marie was being forced to make because of her daughter's schooling. Once the team understood, they offered their support to Marie, telling her that they too had had to make changes in support of their children. With the team's approval, Mike changed Marie's hours so that she could arrive thirty minutes later and leave thirty minutes later, and Marie promised to let the team know in advance if she had to leave early because of a school event.*

You might think that this is an oversimplified example; however, our experience clearly shows that the smallest events are eligible for the use of the scientific method as a means of grasping and resolving a situation. Think of the time and resources the team's members wasted because they did not solve the problem themselves.

To put everything you have learned about how to grasp the situation into perspective, our final story is about a vice president of marketing. Jake White is the featured character in the "Leading Organizational Change" story, which relates how he successfully applied a scientific approach to changing his organization.

Story 14—Leading Organizational Change

by James M. McFillen

This story focuses on Jake White, the division vice president of marketing, and Patrick Sprightly, the company's in-house change agent. The story presents an example of the benefits that can be achieved when you apply the scientific process to a change effort. The story follows the five-step model.

On Wednesday the third, Pat Sprightly received a call from Jake White about setting up an appointment to discuss what Jake described as "an out-of-control problem." During the conversation, Jake mentioned that he was about to send a letter to all key account representatives regarding new customer calls, and he said he wanted to discuss the letter with Pat.

Pat met with Jake and learned, through a series of

questions, that several high-potential customers had called Jake complaining that their key account representatives had not contacted them as Jake had promised they would. These potential customers had waited for three days after speaking with Jake and still had not been contacted. Pat also learned that Jake had an assistant, Nancy Jacobs. Jake was so eager to get going and solve the problem that Pat almost missed his quick reference to Nancy.

Jake got to the point quickly and asked Pat, "Do you believe you can get to the heart of the problem?"

Pat was tempted to express confidence in himself and answer quickly that he believed he could help Jake. However, before he could say that he would help, he needed to assess his own competence and availability. Pat also realized that if he were going to help Jake, he would need to arrange another meeting with Jake and perhaps with the other members of Jake's department who could provide more information and additional perspectives on the situation.

After considering the projects he already had on his plate, Pat told Jake that he would try to help, and Jake agreed to meet with him on the following Monday, the eighth, from 10:00 a.m. until 11:00 a.m. Pat asked if he might also speak with Jake's assistant, Nancy, and Jake agreed. Pat made the arrangements for meeting with Jake and Nancy. Next, he began planning the questions he needed to ask them.

Collecting and Synthesizing Relevant Symptoms

On Monday, Pat met with Jake at the agreed-upon time. They spoke and hammered out some information.

Pat: As I understand it, this situation arose because new customers reported that key account representatives had not called on them as you promised they would do. How many customers are involved?

Jake: First, they are potential customers, not new customers. We expect our key account representatives to make these calls. There are eight potential customers and two account representatives involved.

Pat: Why do you think the calls have not been made?

Jake: These two guys are old-timers who think they are in charge. My guess is that they were out playing golf or something like that.

Pat: How many potential customers called you to complain?

Jake: Three.

Pat: I assume that you assured these potential accounts that you would handle the matter. What did you tell them?

Jake: I promised them that they would receive a call within a day or so.

Pat: After talking with the potential customers, what did you do?

Jake: I told Nancy to get the word out to all key account representatives.

Pat: Is there anything else you think I should know at this point?

Jake: Yes, you are here because my staff recommended you. I need this problem fixed now.

Pat next met with Nancy, Jake's assistant. Pat had to walk to another building to meet with her. She was working in an open office with the order-entry staff. The following dialogue provides a glimpse into the nature of that conversation:

Pat: How did this situation with the potential customers get started?

Nancy: Jake makes promises that can't be met.

Pat: What do you mean?

Nancy: He is like a gunslinger—always shooting from the hip without talking to others.

Pat: What happened in this case?

Nancy: Jake called me a few days ago and told me he wanted all key account representatives put on the alert to be prepared to call on some potential accounts within a few days.

Pat: What did you do?

Nancy: I sent out a letter to all ten key account reps.

Jake: May I have a copy of the letter?

Nancy: Sure, I'll get it for you.

In the course of getting a copy of the letter, Nancy was interrupted by several telephone calls in quick succession. Between the calls, the discussion continued.

Nancy: Some things have come up that I must take care of right now. Can we continue this discussion in a few minutes?

Pat: Well, I need to get back to Jake before I leave and give him a preliminary report. I don't think I'll be able to get back to you until later.

Nancy: Okay! Thanks and good luck.

After meeting with Nancy, Pat was soon ready to get back to the discussion with Jake. Pat met briefly with Jake and explained that he had some ideas but needed to get more information. Jake was dissatisfied with this response and insisted that the situation had to be resolved that day.

By this time, Pat had developed a few ideas about what was taking place, and he believed that Jake was at the center of the issue. To resolve the immediate problem with the three potential customers, Pat suggested that Jake call the two key account representatives and immediately dispatch them to contact the three potential customers. Pat then asked permission to conduct some follow-up discussions with Nancy and all of the key account representatives.

Jake seemed preoccupied. He concluded the brief meeting by saying, "Pat, you write me a proposal, and I'll consider it."

Formulating a Preliminary Diagnosis

Pat quickly developed a proposal for Jake. Pat identified two alternative explanations for the problem with the key account representatives:

- The communication lines between Jake and the key account representatives are breaking down because communications are being funneled through Nancy Jacobs, who is extremely busy.
- The marketing division is being micromanaged because the division does not have a middle tier of management to make the day-to-day decisions.

Instead, upper management is required to make those decisions.

In Pat's proposal, he emphasized the need to determine which of these two explanations was correct. To do this, he planned to collect information from the ten key account representatives as well as from Nancy. He requested permission to interview all ten of the representatives over a two-day period during the following week, and he proposed interviewing Nancy after he had spoken with the account representatives. The questions he planned to ask included the following:

- How does information reach you from upper management?
- When management has a special request for you to call on a potential customer, how long does it take that request to get to you?
- How is the sales division organized?
- What type of management style have you observed in the sales division?

Testing the Preliminary Diagnosis

Jake approved Pat's proposal and requested that Pat begin implementing the interviews as quickly as possible. Pat completed his interviews with the key account representatives and summarized their responses as follows:

How does information from upper management reach account representatives?

Response	Frequency of Response
Through Nancy	9
Directly from Jake	1
During the semiannual sales meetings	7
From the monthly bulletin	6
From weekly activity reports	6
From hearsay and rumors	7

When management has a special request for you to call on a potential customer, how long does it take that request to get to you?

Response	Frequency of Response
One Day	1
Two Days	5
Three Days	3
Four Days	1

How is the sales division organized?

Response	Frequency of Response
Flat	4
Jake and Nancy and the rest of us	2
Unclear	3
I don't know	1

What type of leadership have you observed in the sales division?

Response	Frequency of Response
Top-down	8
Autocratic	9
Micromanagement	10
Controlling	5

In addition, all ten key account representatives made comments. Pat used quotes from the representatives to reflect three major types of responses, and he developed the following frequency analysis of the themes reflected in the interviews:

Typical Comment	Frequency of Comment
"You had better check with all ten account representatives. You'll find that we all have the same problems."	10
"Nancy is like a funnel that all information must go through to reach us. It's not her fault; it's just the way we're organized."	7
"It's time for a change."	8

After a careful review of the above information, Pat concluded that it was necessary to carry out a second phase of data collection involving the entire sales division. Pat notified Jake of the need for additional data because it had not been included in the original proposal. Pat also had to contact Nancy to arrange for her interview.

Jake reluctantly agreed to expand the project to include his entire division. He told Pat that he was concerned that the expanded project might disrupt the work of the sales division. He also commented, "I'm not sure I want to see the results of your survey." Jake provided Pat with some additional information that showed the following makeup of the sales division:

- 98 total people in the sales division
- 3 area managers
- 10 key account representatives
- 7 "inside" staff, including Nancy
- 15 lead managers selected by the sales representatives, one for each of the 15 districts in the United States
- 63 sales managers

Jake also informed Pat that the company operated a bonus system tied primarily to five of the twenty-three products marketed in the United States. Sales over and above the established targets for each of these five products yielded income in addition to base salary.

Based on this additional information, Pat revised his diagnosis to include the following:

- In addition to a breakdown in communications, the bonus system might be influencing the attention being given to potential customers.

- Micromanagement from the top might be a function of both leadership style and organizational design.
- The conflict between the management style of top management and the departmental structure might be causing confusion and distraction.

Pat prepared a questionnaire (see exhibit 1) and sent copies to all ninety-eight members of the sales division. The questionnaire identified each individual's position, length of time in the department, and age.

Exhibit 1
Sales Division Survey

Below are questions concerning the Sales Department. Please circle the number that corresponds to your answer. DO NOT SIGN YOUR NAME.

1. How long does it take for important sales-related information to reach you?

1	2	3	4
one day	two days	three days	more than 3 days

comments:

2. How timely is the sales-related information you receive?

1	2	3	4
always late			very timely

comments:

3. How would you describe the type of management style exhibited by top management?

1	2	3	4
low control			high control

comments:

4. How many organizational levels do you perceive there are in the Sales Department?

1	2	3	4
one level	two levels	three levels	4 levels

comments:

5. How much influence does the bonus system have on your sales efforts?

1	2	3	4
low			high

comments:

Indicate to which group you belong:
◊ Top Management
◊ Area Managers
◊ Key Account Representatives
◊ Inside Staff
◊ Sales Representatives

If you are a Sales Representative, please indicate your district by circling the appropriate number:

1 2 3 4 5 6 7 8 9 10 11 12 13 14 15

Your Age: _____   Years of Service in the Sales Department: _____

The information was to be analyzed and summarized. Feedback would go to Jake and, as Pat put it, "to other individuals not yet identified." The results of the returned surveys are summarized in exhibit 2.

Exhibit 2
Summary of Sales Division Survey Results

Group	Total #	# Returned	Time Lapse 1 day	2 day	3 day	over	Timeliness 1	2	3	4	Management Style 1	2	3	4	Organizational Levels 1	2	3	4	Bonus Influence 1	2	3	4
top management	1	2	2							2		2		2		2	2			2		
area managers	3	3		2	1			2	1				1			2	1				3	
key account reps	10	5			5			1	5				1	4		4	1		3		1	1	4
inside staff	7	6	4	5			1			1			4	2	6		6			3			
sales reps (includes lead manager) by district																						
1	6	1			1		1							1	1				1			1
2	4	3		2				2	1				3			3	1		1		2	1
3	6	5		3	2			3	1			2	3			4	1		1		4	1
4	6	6		4	2			4	2			4	2			5	2		2		5	1
5	6	6		5	1		1	4	1			5	1			4	2		2		4	2
6	4	2		1	1			1					1			1						1
7	3	2		1		1			2					1		1					1	1
8	4	1			1			1	2				2			2	1					1
9	5	3	1	2				1				1	2			4					3	
10	7	2				2	2		2		1		2			1		2	1		2	
11	5	4		2	1			2	2			3	1			1					1	3
12	5	5	1	4			2	1	2			4				4	4				3	2
13	6	5		4	2		2	2	4			2	3			1	4			1	2	3
14	6	6	1	4	2		2	4	3			3	3			1	5			2	1	1
15	5	3		1				2	1				3				3			1	2	5
total	78	54	5	40	22	3	8	29	30	3	1	26	33	10	1	33	34	2	0	10	33	26

Pat scheduled a meeting with Jake and Jake's immediate staff (i.e., the three area managers and Nancy). He decided to organize his feedback for them into three major conclusions, with the first two conclusions each having two parts. Pat's conclusions were as follows:

- 1A. Important information takes an average of two and a half days to reach key account representatives and sales representatives. When it does arrive, it is usually too late to be useful.
- 1B. The bonus system, by keying on five high-priority products, clearly influences the efforts of key account representatives and sales representatives. Some evidence suggests that key account representatives did not jump at the bait because the potential new accounts were not in the market for any of the five high-priority products.
- 2A. A significant number of representatives, staff, and managers believe that upper management micromanages the work of the sales division.
- 2B. The representatives and managers perceive the organizational structure to be relatively flat, with an average of somewhat over two hierarchical levels.
- 3. Confusion appears to exist between the relatively flat structure of the division and the tight control exerted by top management. As one representative put it, "Why do we have area and team leaders if top management is not going to use them as an extension of management?"

Jake and his three area managers accepted Pat's descriptions of the problems, without reservation. Nancy fully agreed with points 2 and 3, but she was very hesitant about agreeing with point 1A. Pat's meeting with Jake and his staff turned into a discussion of how to solve these problems. Everyone appeared to be eager to move forward and "clear up these problems." A number of spontaneous suggestions were made, including, "Let's call everyone in and set the record straight about who is running this division," and "Put bonuses on five more high-priority products," and "Give all the sales representatives computers and use e-mail to communicate with them."

After listening to the discussion and hearing members of the group get their ideas shot down by others, Pat intervened with the following suggestions:

1. "I recommend that you feed back all of the data you have reviewed to the entire division and see if they agree with the conclusions."
2. "If they generally agree, ask for volunteers to work with members of management on project teams for each of the problem areas. We can define their tasks more clearly later to assure that the project teams maintain their focus."
3. "The project teams can explore alternative solutions, present them to management, and gain approval for action."

The first reaction of Jake and his staff was that Pat's proposal would be too time-consuming. However, after further discussion, they reached full agreement to move ahead with Pat's ideas. As the meeting adjourned, the attendees agreed to meet again on Friday at 2:00 p.m. to map out the plan in more detail.

Glenn H. Varney, PhD

Intervention Design

Following the feedback process, three project teams were formed to study the five identified problems and to suggest changes.

Team	Problem(s)	General Issue
1	1A	Information Flow
2	1B	Bonus System
3	2A, 2B, and 3	Organization and Leadership

The project teams met with Jake, Nancy, and the three area managers and made the following recommendations:

1. The marketing division should adopt a team-based structure, as illustrated in exhibit 3.
2. Districts should be consolidated from fifteen to six teams. Team members should select district team leaders. Area managers should become area team coordinators and become part of a marketing division leadership team. This recommendation also included details on roles/job descriptions, organization missions and roles, defined accountability levels, time lines, training, and so on.
3. A computer-based system should be installed to link all district team leaders by e-mail. A beeper system should be provided to each sales representative for immediate access to information via the area team coordinators. A detailed plan for implementing the recommendation was included, covering cost,

schedule, training, support systems, and staffing requirements.

4. The present five-product bonus system should be dismantled and a goal-based program installed in its place. Top management should set the general annual goals. Area team leaders and district team leaders should work with sales teams to establish sales goals. Achievement of above goals for each product should yield a bonus, to be paid annually.

Exhibit 3

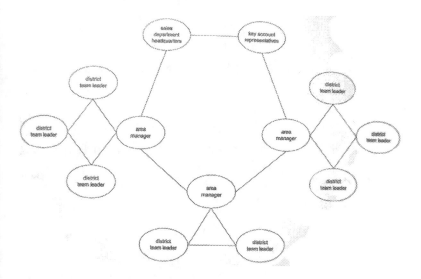

Grasping the Situation after the Fact

Jake's management team accepted the proposed reorganization, and the implementation was completed at an estimated cost of $1 million from start (trigger symptoms) to final installation. Before the change project was undertaken, Jake's sales division was posting the following results:

1. 30 percent of market share
2. 60 key accounts (down from 70 two years earlier)
3. 15 customer complaints per month on average

One year after the new organization was implemented, the marketing division showed the following:

1. 32 percent of market share
2. 75 key accounts
3. 8–9 customer complaints per month on average

Pat was given a promotion for his performance and had only one reservation about what he had accomplished. He wished he had approached the problem from a return-on-investment point of view. He had many people in his organization ask, "How do I know the one-million-dollar investment was worth it?"

HOW TO LEAD CHANGE

Reviewing my consulting files was an interesting and at times challenging journey back through my career. At the time, I found it difficult to admit that my learning experiences had so many bumps and outright flops. I thought I was a smart guy who could learn from a mistake the first time and not have to make it two or three times before the lesson took.

I did finally get it right and realized that applying my good scientist skills when I wanted to change something meant that the first thing I should do was to gather all of the pertinent facts (symptoms) and then sort them into a logical cause-and-effect format. From this format I was next able to develop a descriptive statement (hypothesis) that explained what the problem actually was that needed to be solved. Most importantly, I learned that I had to test my problem description because that is the only way I could be sure what really needed to be changed to correct the problem. Provided that my hypothesis tested valid, meaning that I accurately understood what was going on, then and only then could I design a solution (intervention) that would work. Finally, I measured the results of the intervention to be certain that it was solving the problem I had identified.

In the remainder of this wrap-up, I will summarize all of my learning points and end the book with some general issues and concerns that leaders like you may wish to consider/heed as you journey through your career. Of course I hope that it won't take you as long, or as many mistakes, to learn how to make successful changes as it took me.

There are five categories of learning points arranged in order of importance. The most important, of course, is to *learn how to apply your good scientist skills* to all change efforts.

The second involves your *performance in the role of change agent.*

The third category, and a key issue, is *motivating those affected by the change to want to change* because they can see how they will benefit from the change.

The fourth is making sure that *leaders in the organization are committed to seeing the change through to the end.*

Finally, and perhaps the one least emphasized in my project, is *understanding the culture of the organization*; that is, knowing what the organization is like, what the stakeholders are accustomed to, and what is likely to create resistance to change.

I have summarized each of these five points and provided space for you to record your observations regarding your level of learning and how well you apply it in your organization.

I   Organizational Diagnosis—Applying Your Good Scientist Skills

Always follow these steps when planning change:

- Recognize the symptoms of a present or potential problem.
- Collect information (data) that will help you to understand the problem.
- Develop an explanation of what the problem is (hypothesis).
- Test your hypothesis to make sure that it accurately describes the problem (validating).
- Based on your valid hypothesis, design an intervention that will fix the problem.
- Apply the intervention and measure the results to be sure that the problem is solved.

Here are a few general guidelines that you should consider in making change:

- At the first sign of a problem, slow down. Don't jump right in and try to solve the problem.
- When you first sense a problem, track it down. Don't wait for it to explode into a crisis.
- Put sensing points in place to alert you to impending problems. For example, watch for variances in performance.

- Data/facts/evidence has the power to influence people to change, particularly if it affects them—use it.
- Once you have designed and installed a change, *always* check to make sure it is correcting the problem. Don't assume that it will work.

Change projects succeed more often than not when you properly apply the diagnostic process—your good scientist skills.

How well are you grasping the situation now?

_____

_____

_____

_____

_____

_____

_____

_____

_____

_____

_____

_____

_____

_____

_____

_____

_____

II You as a Change Agent— Regardless of Your Title

Leaders, managers, and supervisors are all change agents, although they usually do not see themselves in that role. Typically they see themselves as controlling, managing, and inspiring staff members to perform effectively and to produce desired results. Yet conditions and the work environment are continually changing, requiring leaders to oversee and effectively manage change.

Here are a few lessons we learned about leading change and grasping the situation:

- Never try to change anything without the full awareness of all the stakeholders, as well as their support and commitment to the change.
- As you are making the change, continuously take the pulse of the top leaders to be sure that they remain committed to the change.
- When you doubt your own commitment and support for the change, don't try to implement it—it will fail.
- Don't fall into the trap of feeling infallible, believing that you can do almost anything and make it work.
- Sometimes you may be motivated to make change because you think you will receive positive recognition, a promotion, or a raise. Be careful of this motivation; it is easy to fall into this mind-set.
- Be wary if you think you know all there is to know about human behavior. Be careful not to classify people the way we did with Harold the Horrible.

- Before you undertake any change, make sure that your top leadership knows where you are planning to take them.
- Be attentive to your top leaders and hold their hands to reassure them that you know what you are doing.
- Foster open-mindedness; try to keep the stakeholders from jumping to conclusions before all of the facts are in.

How many of these nine points are you already applying?

_____

_____

_____

_____

_____

_____

_____

_____

_____

_____

_____

_____

_____

_____

_____

_____

_____

III Motivating the Troops to Change

As a general rule, people don't like to change. They are comfortable and like the things the way they are, and they are usually ready to resist change efforts. If you try to initiate change without forewarning and involving them, don't be surprised if they resist your efforts.

Here are a few ways to get the troops on board, thus avoiding foot dragging and out-and-out resistance:

- Always engage the stakeholders in the diagnostic and planning stages of change.
- When stakeholders are engaged in designing the change intervention, they will feel a sense of ownership and support for the change.
- Seek out and engage *all* of the stakeholders. Be careful not to overlook some distant leader, an isolated group, or perhaps even a customer. They can scuttle your change project.
- Simply asking for someone's opinion can help to get them engaged from the start.
- Don't expect people to be receptive to learning something new if they don't feel the need to change something they are comfortable doing.

Where are you on motivating the troops?

_____

_____

_____

_____

_____

Glenn H. Varney, PhD

_____

_____

_____

_____

_____

_____

_____

_____

_____

_____

_____

_____

IV Getting Leaders to Lead

Leaders at the top of the organization who were not committed to the change negatively affected a number of our projects. They were willing to allow us to attempt change because they thought it was a good thing to do or because they had heard of some other organization doing it. Usually it was a flavor of the month that the leader at the top of the organization had been told about or read about in some magazine. Often their approach was "We'll just give it a try and see what happens. After all, what can it hurt?"

Here are some straightforward ideas to help avoid leader disengagement:

- Never decide to implement a change just because it worked for someone else. If you think it might be good for your organization, then test it in your organization to see its effect before you go into it whole hog.
- If your test run is positive, show all the stakeholders how it will benefit them.
- Watch out for leaders who return from a conference or a seminar hell-bent on implementing someone else's hot-button idea. It's easy to go along with them, but stand your ground and test before you implement.

Glenn H. Varney, PhD

How much of a problem will this be for you?

_____

_____

_____

_____

_____

_____

_____

_____

_____

_____

_____

_____

_____

V   Know the Organizational Culture

Culture is a broad term used to describe what an organization is like. It can tell you what people are accustomed to and what they like about their organization. It can help you to identify which changes are likely to work and which ones won't. Trying to force change into an organization is a recipe for failure. For example, if you introduce people into a group whose culture is radically different from those already in the group, you can expect resistance and even rejection of the new people. Story 12, "The Diagnostic Process Worked but Was Then Forgotten," is a good example of what happens when you ignore cultural fit.

Always study and understand your organization's culture before you undertake major change. For more information on culture, we recommend:

Organizational Culture and Leadership by Edgar H. Schein (Jossey-Bass, 3rd ed., 2004).

How would you describe your organization's culture?

_____

_____

_____

_____

_____

_____

_____

_____

_____

Glenn H. Varney, PhD

_____

_____

_____

_____

_____

_____

_____

_____

Conclusion

Looking back at our career journey revealed that there were a few side trips that were not in the mainstream of our learning. Some of these issues and concerns can be controversial, and you might not agree with our points of view. That's okay; they are intended to be food for thought. We reached these conclusions during our travels but not without many experiences to reinforce our beliefs.

- *Most* leadership and management training programs are not very valuable because they are not based on the needs or problems of the people being trained. These programs do not take into consideration the organizations from which the participants come or the potential that the participants have of practicing what is being taught when they get back home.
- The great majority of consultants are in it for the money and have no real idea of whether or not their hot-button idea will really change anything, much less human behavior.
- Too many leaders have fallen in love with the way they are doing things now, and they have no interest in listening to anyone else's ideas.
- Leaders might be in support of a change and its design but have no idea how this change will affect others in the organization and how those others might react. Consequently, they really don't know if the change will achieve the desired result.
- When the human resources department gets involved, it most often muddies the waters, making things more difficult.

- Why many technically oriented leaders don't apply their good scientist skills to problem solving and change is a mystery to us.
- The diagnostic process works in almost any situation, but *many* consultants and leaders disagree with us about this.
- Some (too many) leaders and consultants see themselves as know-it-alls. They have no interest in what the facts and data may say about the situation.
- There are too many quick-draw leaders in organizations. They jump to conclusions without the evidence to support those conclusions.

That's it, folks. Just remember to use your good scientist skills and the following steps in the scientific process to make sure that you grasp the situation before you change anything.

Hopefully you followed the ups and downs of our learning process and will remember the following:

1. Always *recognize the problem* before you make any changes.
2. You do this by *collecting and synthesizing relevant symptoms of the problem.*
3. After you have collected and organized the data, then *formulate a preliminary diagnosis.*
4. Next you should *test the preliminary diagnosis* to be sure that you thoroughly understand the problem.
5. Finally, you are ready to *design an intervention* that will correct the problem.

Here's hoping your own adventures in change management are productive and successful. I wish you the best of success in your career.

Appendix

Glenn H. Varney, PhD

Journal of Change Management
iFirst article, 1–24, 2012

Organizational Diagnosis:
An Evidence-based Approach

JAMES M. MCFILLEN*, DEBORAH A. O'NEIL*, WILLIAM K.
BALZER** & GLENN H. VARNEY*

*Department of Management, Bowling Green State University, Bowling Green, OH, USA, **Department of Psychology, Bowling Green State University, Bowling Green, OH, USA

ABSTRACT *Organizational diagnosis plays a critical role in organizational change initiatives in terms of both choosing appropriate interventions and contributing to readiness-to-change within an organization. Although numerous authors identify diagnosis as an integral component of the change process and many have recommended specific theories and models that should be used in diagnosis, little attention has been given to the diagnostic process itself. The lack of rigour in the diagnostic process and the misdiagnoses that follow are likely to be significant factors in the high failure rate of change initiatives reported in the literature. This article reviews evidence-based diagnosis in engineering and medicine, summarizes the basic steps found in those diagnostic processes, identifies three cause–effect relationships that underlie evidence-based diagnosis, and suggests four spheres of knowledge that must intersect to guide the diagnostic process. Based upon that review, an evidence-based approach for organizational diagnosis is proposed with the goals of bringing more scientific rigour to the diagnostic process, improving the appropriateness of interventions chosen for a given situation and contributing to readiness-to-change among organizational members. Finally, specific steps are recommended for advancing the state of organizational diagnosis in the field of organization development and change.*

KEY WORDS: Organizational diagnosis, organization development, change management, evidence-based diagnosis, organizational diagnosis model

Correspondence Address: James M. McFillen, Department of Management, College of Business Administration, Bowling Green State University, Bowling Green, OH 43403, USA. Email: jmcfill@bgsu.edu

1469-7017 Print/1479-1811 Online/12/000001–24 © 2012 Taylor & Francis
http://dx.doi.org/10.1080/14697017.2012.679290

Open Book Editions
A Berrett-Koehler Partner

Open Book Editions is a joint venture between Berrett-Koehler Publishers and Author Solutions, the market leader in self-publishing. There are many more aspiring authors who share Berrett-Koehler's mission than we can sustainably publish. To serve these authors, Open Book Editions offers a comprehensive self-publishing opportunity.

A Shared Mission

Open Book Editions welcomes authors who share the Berrett-Koehler mission—Creating a World That Works for All. We believe that to truly create a better world, action is needed at all levels—individual, organizational, and societal. At the individual level, our publications help people align their lives with their values and with their aspirations for a better world. At the organizational level, we promote progressive leadership and management practices, socially responsible approaches to business, and humane and effective organizations. At the societal level, we publish content that advances social and economic justice, shared prosperity, sustainability, and new solutions to national and global issues.

Open Book Editions represents a new way to further the BK mission and expand our community. We look forward to helping more authors challenge conventional thinking, introduce new ideas, and foster positive change.

For more information, see the Open Book Editions website:
http://www.iuniverse.com/Packages/OpenBookEditions.aspx

Join the BK Community! See exclusive author videos, join discussion groups, find out about upcoming events, read author blogs, and much more! http://bkcommunity.com/

Printed in the United States
By Bookmasters